Principles of Communication

Charles Nandi

Reference Press

4831/24, Ansari Road,
Darya Ganj,
New Delhi-110 002.
Phone: 51563444, 23260807
Fax: 51563334
E-mail: info@essessreference.com
url: www.essessreference.com

First Published : 2006

Rs.550/-

ISBN: 81-8405-007-0

Published By:
Reference Press
4831/24, Ansari Road,
Darya Ganj,
New Delhi-110 002.
Phone: 23260807, 51563444
Fax: 51563334
E-mail: info@essessreference.com
url: www.essessreference.com

Printed in India at:
Mehra Offset Press, New Delhi.

Contents

Preface

Communication can be interactive, transactive, intentional or unintentional; it can also be verbal or non verbal. Communication varies considerably in form and style when considering scale. Internal communication, within oneself is intrapersonal while communication between two persons is interpersonal. At larger scales of communication, both the systems of communication and the media of communication changes. Small group communication takes place in settings of between three and twelve individuals creating a different set of interactions than large groups such as organizational communication in settings like companies or communities. At the largest scales, mass communication described communication to huge numbers of individuals through mass media. Communication also has a time component, being either synchronous or asynchronous. There are a number of theories of communication that attempt to explain human communication.

This book uses modern principles of communication systems such as the compact discs, television, the telephone and the computer as the motivation for you to study their basic principles. From analog to digital conversion, spectrum and bandwidth and packet and circuit switching, to electricity and electronics, modulation and multiplexing and computer processing, the author takes a thorough and phased approach in presenting major topics.

Structured in modular format, the book covers audio technology, video systems, speech communication systems and written communication systems, applying key concepts in each area to real world communication systems.

An easy to comprehend book, that gives the reader a complete introduction to communication technologies and systems, offering you a solid understanding of the fundamentals, history and the future direction of this ever changing field. Geared towards non-technical business professionals and students, this unique resource integrates human physiology and factors, important inventors & business people and basic technological principles to explain the key concepts and developments of modern principles of communication.

I shall like to thank all those who helped me in writing of this book, this would not have been possible without the support of my daughter Junie, wife Sucheta, mother Mrs. Putul Nandi and father Mr. S.K. Nandi. I shall be failing in my duty if I don't thank Prof. Dr. Tapati Basu, Head, Department of Journalism, Mass Communication and Media Studies, University of Calcutta.

Jhansi **Charles Nandi**
November, 2005

1

Introduction

For communication to take place, there must be a sender, a message, a means of sending that message and a receiver. The sender creates and sends a message verbally, on paper, electronically or through visual means. The receiver gets the message, interprets it and acts upon it. Most people aren't aware of this sequence as they're using it. But if a message isn't properly received, knowing the separate steps enables the sender to backtrack and find out where the cycle broke down. In other words, the whole cycle must be completed for every successful communication.

Modes of Communication

Communications are flexible. Once the content of a message is set, there are four different ways of sending it. Deciding which one to use is as much a part of effective communications as actually using it. The key is to choose the mode of communication that is most convenient and effective under a particular set of circumstances.

Oral Communications

Face-to-face, over the telephone, on radio or on television, the spoken word is one of the most versatile modes of communication. From conversations and meetings to training sessions, oral communications are ideal when a lot of information needs to be exchanged between the sender and the receiver. The whole cycle can be completed quickly, information is exchanged freely, and other tasks can be performed during the exchange.

Written Communications

Written communication is a slower, more measured exchange of information. If a joint committee is recommending ways to correct a hazardous condition in the workplace, written communication is essential, because descriptions, diagrams and specifications are likely to be more precise. Written communications also provide a permanent record of important information.

Visual Communications

Visual communications such as charts, graphs, pictures, illustrations or videos, are usually an aid to effective communication, because they illustrate or show information instead of explaining it with words alone. Used together, written and visual communications can often promote better understanding on the part of the person receiving the message.

Body Language

Faces and bodies are indirect factors in communications, but they can directly affect the quality of the message. In any oral communication, body movements and gestures can support or contradict what is being said. Tone of voice and emphasis also add meaning. Since a high percentage of understanding comes from non-verbal clues, it is important to the sender to be sure that body language supports the message, and does not become a barrier.

Combinations

The most effective communications are those that use more than one mode, and therefore more than one human sense. Studies have shown that people retain only 20 percent of what they hear, and only 30 percent of what they read. When people both hear and read information, the total percentage of information retained rises to 50 percent. A good program, for instance, might start with a short oral introduction, illustrate the message with a video presentation, follow it with a discussion, and close with reference to a written text or manual.

Listening

A common error is to think of communications only in terms of sending written or verbal messages. The best communications are two-way. The ability to listen carefully with an open mind —rather than just hearing—is one of the most important communication skills.

COMMUNICATION TECHNIQUES

Skills are needed to make the best use of each communications mode. Most communication skills are a combination of common sense and basic grammar and vocabulary.

Oral Communication

- The certified member needs effective oral communication techniques. A thorough knowledge of those techniques is also essential when it comes to evaluating workplace training programs.
- Effective oral communication starts before a word has been spoken. Positive body language, good eye contact and a warm tone of voice help ensure that the

audience - whether it is one person or a group—never feels talked down to and stays interested.

- Oral messages should be kept simple. Big, complex words can be confusing. Different cultural meanings of certain words should be checked to make sure no one is offended. Jargon should not be used unless the communicator is sure that the listener understands it.

Effective Listening

- Good listening is not just an important communication skill. It is also one of the most difficult and the most neglected.
- The first step in effective listening is to pay close attention to what the speaker is saying and to listen to the whole ideas, not just the individual words. By keeping distractions to a minimum, the listener stays focused and lets the speaker know the message is of interest.
- Listening is not passive. Active listeners make better communicators. At the end of the message they may ask open-ended questions to obtain more information and to keep the discussion focused. When the speaker has finished, the active listeners may repeat the message in their own words to show that it was correctly understood.
- Good listening means keeping an open mind. Personal likes or dislikes of the sender or the subject of the message must be put aside. Listening to the whole message before making a judgment is essential.

Written Communication

- To some people, the prospect of writing can be intimidating. Writing requires more specialized skills than speaking. However, good writing in a report on health and safety questions should not prove difficult. It must simply be clear, direct and well organized. An understanding of the basic elements of writing - words, sentences, paragraphs and headings - can help.

- When writing, words should be chosen with care. They should be familiar, preferably short, gender-neutral if possible and non-technical unless those who will read the report are familiar with the technical language or jargon. Often several words have a similar meaning; the writer should try to select the one that describes the thought most precisely.
- Sentences should be kept short and each sentence should contain only one idea. Avoid excess words and phrases. For example, the word if takes up a lot less room than the phrase in the event that; yet their meanings are identical.
- Paragraphs organize information into a logical order. Short paragraphs are best and should be limited to one topic or part of a topic. The first sentence of the paragraph should introduce the idea, and the remaining sentences provide detail.
- Before starting to write, it is often useful to make a plan or outline. The outline divides the report into main sections with major headings. The outline keeps the report organized by dividing the material into sections.

Reports

A badly written report—say an inspection report—wastes the work the committee member has already put in. Information has been gathered, the physical inspection completed and the results noted and analyzed. Conclusions have been drawn and recommendations carefully considered. A badly organized or poorly written report may turn an otherwise effective and thorough process into an unreadable and confusing puzzle. A carefully organized and well-written report presents that work and those recommendations in a persuasive and convincing way. It should state the gathered information precisely, noting the results of the inspection and any conclusions and recommendations that have been considered.

In preparing a report, the writer should apply the writing techniques described here to the following five-part structure or outline.

Introduction and purpose

This section introduces the report and generally explains what is contained in the report and its purpose.

Methods

The second section describes the methods used to gather the information or observations.

Findings

A review of the information gathered and observations made are contained in this section. For clarity, information may be divided into categories. An accident investigation report, for instance, might contain the following sub-sections:

- a brief description of accident or incident;
- the names of persons interviewed or contacted;
- the causes of accident or incident.
- Conclusions

This section contains a statement of the underlying cause of a given situation, in the opinion of the writer, based on the data which were gathered and analysed. Each conclusion should be separately identified and explained. Where the report reflects the consensus of the JHSC, this should be indicated.

Recommendations

Recommendations flow from the conclusions. They are specific proposals for decisions or actions. They must be clearly stated. Introduction, method, findings, conclusions and recommendations make up the body of the report. The following two kinds of attachments may be useful as well.

Supporting Documentation

Other documents which provide information that has been considered in the report should be attached. This might include an official report from a recognized authority. The main conclusion drawn from this official report can be explained in the findings or conclusions with a note that a copy of the original is attached.

Bibliography

In some cases, the employer or other person receiving a report will want to check original sources that are described or referred to in the report. If copies of these sources are not attached to the report, a bibliography should be attached, to show the reader where this material can be obtained. Each reference should include title, author and publisher and where the material can be found.

Workplace Communication Tools

Workplace communications can be enhanced with a variety of practical tools.

Bulletin Boards

Bulletin boards are useful for communicating health and safety information because people are used to checking them. Bulletins should have a simple layout, a large headline and a very brief message. Bulletin boards are not appropriate for communicating lengthy or detailed information.

Posters

Posters can also be used to quickly call attention to an issue. Larger than a bulletin, they use illustrations and slogans instead of text to get across simple ideas: for example, the importance of reading WHMIS labels.

Newsletters

Newsletters provide a permanent record of information that can be read at leisure outside the workplace. Like any other formal publication, they need a name to establish continuity from one issue to the next. Newsletters can often be produced in the workplace.

Safety Talks

Safety talks can involve a small group of people from a specific part of the workplace. These personal presentations by JHSC members encourage feedback that may in itself suggest topics for future talks.

Special Bulletins

Special bulletins, sometimes called flash reports, are designed to communicate urgent information when other channels are too slow. The design should be accordingly different so that flash reports are not ignored or lost amongst other information.

Training

One of the most important applications of communication skills is in the design and evaluation of workplace training programs. Adult education is an integral part of building awareness of occupational health and safety. When developing training programs, it is important to remember how adults learn and to make the most of the many strengths they bring to the process. Successful adult learning depends on some basic principles:

- New concepts and information should relate back to the life and work experience of the adults involved, as far as possible.
- Facts and ideas must not be presented in a narrow or rigid framework.
- Good or bad past learning experiences affect how adults learn.
- The work and life experience of adults must be recognized and reinforced as an advantage in training.
- The motivation of adults, who are volunteer participants, should also be taken into account in the preparation and presentation of training.

Adults learn best what is most relevant or most needed. New information and skills are accepted sooner if trainees can relate them immediately and directly to actual health and safety issues they deal with at work. Participants have different approaches to learning and problem solving. Learning can be divided into four stages: feeling or experience; observation (as a result of experience); thought (developing new theories about that experience); and action (testing the theory in an everyday situation). Since some people learn more at one stage than another, the program should feature all four stages. The learning atmosphere is improved when a variety of techniques is used.

Adults learn more when they participate in the process. A one-sided lecture is less effective because the participants have no control over the learning process. Training should be interactive or two-way, based on cooperation and discussion between trainer and trainee.

Learning is the result of experience and practice. Skills that are practiced are retained sooner and for longer. Adults don't change behaviour patterns because they're told to. They accept something when they can see for themselves that it works. Training programs should include opportunities for participants to experiment with new facts and concepts.

Learning is an emotional and intellectual process. Adults don't learn unless they believe or feel that what is being presented is correct and relevant. Programs must be centred on the participants themselves rather than a specific task or piece of information. Adult motivation to learn is usually strong in this kind of environment.

Objectives are important. By setting goals, participants know where learning is headed. Frequent opportunities to check progress against those goals should be built into the program.

Educational Tools

Educational tools are instruments that help participants to learn and retain information. Tools should never be used simply to replace interaction between instructor and participants or to fill in time. Their purpose is to enhance the learning experience and save time. Some of the most commonly used educational tools are described briefly here.

Printed materials range from participant and instructor manuals outlining the course content to reference materials and handouts. Handouts may include case studies, problems and quizzes that provide background to group discussions or workshops. Audio tools are usually recordings. In a health and safety context, they are most often used to study problems associated with noise. As a rule, they work better when they are combined with visual aids.

Flip charts, chalkboards and whiteboards are traditional visual tools. All are useful for recording ideas during brainstorming sessions. They can also be used to draw flow charts or diagrams that illustrate an idea. Flip charts are most flexible, because they can be used as permanent records during the program. Overhead and slide projectors provide a larger, brighter image than boards or flip charts, using slides and transparencies that are either ready-made or written out during the session.

Audio-visual aids combine sight and sound. The most popular of these is videotape because of its familiarity to participants and ease of operation. Although videotapes are not interactive, they are useful for bringing all participants up to speed on a given subject at the beginning of a program. Throughout the program, they can illustrate practical applications of a given theory. Videotapes can also be used to show events that cannot be readily performed in a classroom.

2

Process of Communication

Communication is the process of exchanging information usually via a common system of symbols. "Communication studies" is the academic discipline that studies communication.

Components of Human Communication

Humans communicate in order to share knowledge and experiences. Common forms of human communication include sign language, speaking, writing, gestures, and broadcasting. Communication can be interactive, transactive, intentional, or unintentional; it can also be verbal or nonverbal. Communication varies considerably in form and style when considering scale. Internal communication, within oneself, is intrapersonal while communication between two individuals is interpersonal.

At larger scales of communication both the system of communication and media of communication change. Small group communication takes place in settings of between three and 12 individuals creating a different set of interactions than large groups such as organizational communication in settings like companies or communities. At the largest scales mass communication describes communication to huge numbers of individuals through mass media. Communication also has a time component, being either synchronous or asynchronous. There are a number of theories of communication that attempt to explain human communication.

Communication Technology

In telecommunications, the first transatlantic two-way radio broadcast occurred on July 25th 1920. As the technology evolved, communication protocol also had to evolve; for example, Thomas Edison had to discover that hello was the least ambiguous greeting by voice over a distance; previous greetings such as hail tended to be lost or garbled in the transmission. As regards human communication these diverse fields can be divided into those which cultivate a thoughtful exchange between a small number of people (debate, talk radio, e-mail, personal letters) on the one hand; and those which disseminate broadly a simple message (Public relations, television, cinema).

Our indebtedness to the Ancient Romans in the field of communication does not end with the Latin root "communicare". They devised what might be described as the first real mail or postal system in order to centralize control of the empire from Rome. This allowed Rome to gather knowledge about events in its many widespread provinces. As the Romans well knew, communication is as much about taking in towards the centre as it is about putting out towards the extremes.

In virtual management an important issue is computer-mediated communication. The view people take toward communication is changing, as new technologies change the way they communicate and organize. In fact, it is the changing technology of communication that tends to make the most frequent and widespread changes in a society - take for example the rise of web cam chat and other network-based visual communications between distant parties. The latest trend in communication, decentralized personal networking, is termed smartmobbing.

Communication Barriers

Anxiety associated with communication is known as communication apprehension. Such anxiety tends to be influenced by one's self-concept. Besides apprehension, communication can be impaired via bypassing, indiscrimination, and polarization. Failing to share a common language is also an important barrier in many parts of the world.

Knowledge Visualization

Knowledge visualization, "the use of visual representations to transfer knowledge between at least two persons", aims to improve the transfer of knowledge by using computer and non-computerbased visualization methods complementary. Examples of such visual formats are sketches, diagrams, images, objects, interactive visualizations, information visualization applications, imaginary visualizations, stories. While information visualization (IV) concentrates on the use of computer-supported tools to derive new insights, knowledge visualization (KV) focuses to transfer insights and to create new knowledge in groups.

Beyond the mere transfer of facts, knowledge visualization aims to further transfer insights, experiences, attitudes, values, expectations, perspectives, opinions, and predictions by using various complementary visualizations. Knowledge Visualization has it's roots in Visual Com issue to make knowledge visible so that it can be better identified, accessed, shared, discussed, applied, or generally be managed.

Communications Satellite

A communications satellite (sometimes abbreviated to comsat) is an artificial satellite stationed in space for the purposes of telecommunications or reconnaisance using radio at microwave frequencies. Most communications satellites use geosynchronous orbits or near-geostationary orbits, although some recent systems use low Earth-orbiting satellites. A location on the ground with satellite dishes used to transmit to or receive from these is called an earth station or teleport.

Communications satellites provide a technology that is complementary to that of fiber optic submarine communication cables. Unlike fiber optic communication, satellite communication has a propagation delay (also called a path delay) of at least 270 milliseconds, which is the time it takes the radio signal to travel 35,800 km from earth to a satellite and then back to earth. Satellite Internet connections average a 600 to 800 millisecond delay, about ten times that of a terrestrial Internet link. This delay is a challenge for highly interactive applications such as video phones, VOIP or real-time online video games.

History of Communications Satellite

The concept of the geosynchonous communications satellite was first proposed by Arthur C. Clarke, building on work by Konstantin Tsiolkovsky and on the 1929 work by Herman Potocnik (writing as Herman Noordung) "Das Problem der Befahrung des Weltraums - der Raketen-motor". In October 1945 Clarke published an article titled "[Extra-terrestrial Relays]" in the British magazine Wireless

World. The article described the fundamentals behind the deployment of artificial satellites in geostationary orbits for the purpose of relaying radio signals. Thus Arthur C. Clarke is often quoted as being the inventor of the communications satellite.

The first satellite to relay communications was Project SCORE in 1958, which used a tape recorder to store and forward voice messages. It was used to send a Christmas greeting to the world from President Eisenhower. NASA launched an Echo satellite in 1960. This 100 foot aluminized Mylar balloon served as a passive reflector for radio communications. Telstar was the first active, direct relay communications satellite. Belonging to AT&T as part of a multi-national agreement between AT&T, Bell Telephone Laboratories, NASA, the British General Post Office, and the French National PTT (Post Office) to develop satellite communication, it was launched by NASA from Cape Canaveral on July 10, 1962, the first privately sponsored space launch. Telstar was placed in an elliptical orbit (completed once every 2 hours and 37 minutes), rotating at a 45° angle above the equator.

The first geosynchronous communications satellite was Hughes' Syncom 2, launched on July 26, 1963. However, Syncom 2 was positioned in an inclined orbit, so special tracking equipment was needed to see it. The first geosynchronous communications satellite that could be seen from a fixed satellite antenna (over North America) was Anik 1, a Canadian satellite launched in 1973. This class of satellite was spin-scan stabilized, meaning that the satellite's antennas could receive/transmit useful information from/to Earth regardless of the position of its solar-cell arrays. The United States launched their own geosynchronous communication satellites afterward, with Western Union launching their Westar 1 satellite in 1974, and RCA Americom launching Satcom 1 in 1975.

It was Satcom 1 that was instrumental in helping early cable TV channels such as WTBS (now TBS Superstation), HBO, CBN (now ABC Family Channel), and The Weather Channel become successful, because these channels distributed their programming to all of the local cable TV headends using the satellite. Additionally, it was the first satellite used by broadcast TV networks in the USA, like ABC, NBC, and CBS, to distribute their programming to all of their local affiliate stations. The reason that Satcom 1 was so widely used is because it had twice the communications capacity of Westar 1 (24 transponders as opposed to Westar 1's 12), which resulted in less transponder usage costs.

By 2000 Hughes Space Systems, now part of Boeing, had built nearly 40 percent of the satellites in service worldwide.

LEOs

A low Earth orbiting satellite is a satellite with a low orbit and an orbital period significantly less than a day. As these satellites can only be seen from any given part of the Earth for a short time as they pass over, large numbers of these satellites are needed to ensure continuous coverage. A group of satellites working in concert thus is known as a satellite constellation. Examples of satellite constellations are the GPS and the Iridium and Globalstar satellite telephony services.

It is possible to offer discontinuous coverage using a low Earth orbit satellite capable of storing data received while passing over one part of Earth and transmitting it later while passing over another part. This will be the case with the CASCADE system of Canada's CASSIOPE communications satellite.

Television

A direct broadcast satellite is a special high-powered communications satellite that transmits to small DBS satellite dishes. Direct broadcast satellites generally operate in the upper portion of the Ku band. Other frequency bands include the original C band, Ku band, and eventually Ka band. See broadcast satellites for further information.

Amateur Radio

Amateur Radio operators have access to the OSCAR satellites that have been designed specifically to carry amateur radio traffic. Most such satellites operate as spaceborne repeaters, and are generally accessed by amateurs equipped with UHF or VHF radio equipment and highly directional antennas such as Yagis or dish antennas. Due to the limitations of ground-based amateur equipment, most amateur satellites are launched into fairly low earth orbits, and are designed to deal with only a limited number of brief contacts at any given time. Some satellites also provide data-forwarding services using the AX.25 or similar protocols.

Telecommunication

Telecommunication is the extension of communication over a distance. In practice it also recognizes that something may be lost in the process; hence the term 'telecommunication' covers all forms of distance and/or conversion of the original communications, including radio, telegraphy, television, telephony, data communication and computer networking.

The elements of a telecommunication system are a transmitter, a medium (line) and possibly a channel imposed upon the medium, and a receiver. The transmitter is a device that transforms or encodes the message into a physical phenomenon; the signal. The transmission medium, by its physical nature, is likely to modify or degrade the signal on its path from the transmitter to the receiver. The receiver has a decoding mechanism capable of recovering the message within certain limits of signal degradation. In some cases, the final "receiver" is the human eye and/or ear (or in some extreme cases other sense organs) and the recovery of the message is done by the brain.

Telecommunication can be point-to-point, point-to-multipoint or broadcasting, which is a particular form of point-to-multipoint that goes only from the transmitter to the receivers. One of the roles of the telecommunications engineer is to analyse the physical properties of the line or transmission medium, and the statistical properties of the message in order to design the most effective encoding and decoding mechanisms.

When systems are designed to communicate through human sense organs (mainly vision and hearing), physiological and psychological characteristics of human perception will be taken into account. This has important economic implications and engineers will research what defects may be tolerated in the signal yet not affect the viewing or hearing experience too badly.

Examples of human (tele)communications

In a simplistic example, consider a normal conversation between two people. The message is the sentence that the speaker decides to communicate to the listener. The transmitter is the language areas in the brain, the motor cortex, the vocal cords, the larynx, and the mouth that produce those sounds called speech. The signal is the sound waves (pressure fluctuations in air particles) that can be identified as speech. The channel is the air carrying those sound waves, and all the acoustic properties of the surrounding space: echoes, ambient noise, reverberation.

Between the speaker and the listener (the receiver), might be other devices that do or do not introduce their own distortions of the original vocal signal (e.g. telephone, HAM radio, IP phone, etc.) The penultimate receiver is the listener's ear and auditory system, the auditory nerve, and the language areas in the listener's brain that will "decode" the signal into meaningful information and filter out background noise.

All channels have noise. Another important aspect of the channel is called the bandwidth. A low bandwidth channel, such as a telephone, cannot carry all of the audio information that is transmitted in normal conversation, causing distortion and irregularities in the speaker's voice, as compared to normal, in-person speech.

3

Interpersonal Communication

Interpersonal communication refers to communication with another person. This kind of communication is subdivided into dyadic communication, public communication, and small-group communication.

Interpersonal communication encompasses:

— Speech

— Nonverbal communication

— Unconscious communication

— summarizing

— paraphrasing

Having good interpersonal communication skills support such processes as:

— selling

— counselling

— coaching

— mentoring and co-mentoring, which is mentoring in groups

— conflict resolution

Interpersonal communication is the subject of a number of disciplines in thee field of psychology, notably Transactional analysis. It can be affected by a communication disorder or by arrogance, shyness, etc.

Speech:

— (n.) an oral presentation by one person to a group (or sometimes just an individual); closely related terms include:

— Conversation (infomal speech by more than one person on a topic),

— Debate (formal communication between two groups holding opposing views before an audience), and

— the academic discipline of communications.

— (v.) the act of producing voice through the use of the vocal cords or other means, such as sign language, to create linguistic acts that communicate information from an initiator to a recipient. Synonyms for the verb usage include talk, say, oral, speak, tell, oral; verbal includes written communication.

In more colloquial terms, speech can be described in several different ways:

1. A linguistic act designed to convey information orally.
2. Various linguistic acts where the audience includes more than one individual, including public speaking, oration, and quotation.
3. The physical act of speaking, primarily through the use of vocal chords to produce voice.

However, speech can also take place inside one's head, known as intrapersonal communication, for example, when one thinks or utters sounds of approval or disapproval. At a deeper level, one could even consider subconscious processes, including dreams where aspects of oneself communicate with each other (see Sigmund Freud), as part of intrapersonal communication, even though most human beings do not seem to have direct access to such communication.

There are several factors that can affect the clarity of speech as such. Among these are:

1. Diseases and disorders of the lungs or the vocal cords, including paralysis, respiratory infections, and cancers of the lungs and throat.
2. Diseases and disorders of the brain, including alogia, aphasias and speech processing disorders, where impaired perception of the message (as opposed to the actual sound) leads to poor speech production.
3. Articulatory problems, such as stuttering, lisping, cleft palate, ataxia, or nerve damage leading to problems in articulation. Tourette syndrome and nervous tics can also affect speech.
4. Problems in the perception of sound and auditory information can affect speech. In addition to aphasias, anomia and certain types of dyslexia can impede the quality of auditory perception, and therefore, expression. Hearing impairments and deafness can be considered to fall into this category.

Thus, it is clear that speech has both expressive and receptive elements. The purpose of speech can be to convey meaning or to increase social bonds between individuals and/or groups (it is often both). For the latter shallowness is not a problem. The success of a speech act depends on numerous factors, including the presence or absence of a variety of speech disorders, the ability of the speaker to express the intended message, and the ability and willingness of the audience to play the role of recipient.

Nonverbal Communication

Often defined as communication without words, nonverbal communication (NVC) refers to all aspects of a message which are not conveyed by the literal meaning of words. Both written and spoken communication can be nonverbal. The main types of NVC are chronemics, kinesics, paralinguistics, proxemics and semiotics. Culture, gender and social status influence nonverbal communication. NVC also includes object communication and haptics or touch.

Chronemics refers to how people use and interperet time. Kinesics refers to what people often call body language and includes facial expressions, gestures, posture and eye contact. Paralinguistics is the sound element of nonverbal communication. (See paralanguage.)

Object Communication

The most common form of object communication is clothing. The type of clothing that a person wears are often used to determine their personality traits, though this is considered a form of stereotyping. Social groups often use a common form of clothing to set themselves apart from other, presumably unaligned social groups. A good example of clothing as object communication is thee uniform.

Object communication extends beyond clothing to other body adornments, such as wedding rings or bindis to indicate marital status, tattoos, piercings, and brands. Also included in object communication is anything used as a status symbol.

Unconscious Communication

Unconscious communication (or intuitive) is the transfer of information unconsciously between humans. It is sometimes intrapersonal, like dreaming or cognition under the effects of hypnosis.

Due to the Magical Number Seven our conscious attention can attend to 5-9 objects simultaneously. All other information is processed by thee unconscious mind. Usually our unconscious communication and unconscious behaviour are influenced and/or dictated by our culture. Communication between people of different cultures and subcultures can sometimes cause unexpected suffering and conflicts. Understanding of unconscious communication can avoid such conflicts. Unconscious communication can cause changes in mood or emotion.

Sales

Sales, or the activity of selling, forms an integral part of commercial activity. Mastering sales is considered by many as some sort of persuading "art". On the contrary, the methodological approach of selling, refers to it as a systematic process of repetitive and measurable milestones, by which a salesperson relate his offering enabling the buyer to visualize how to achieve his goal in an economic way. Selling is a practical implementation of marketing, it often forms a separate grouping in a corporate structure, employing separate specialist operatives known as salesmen (singular: salesman or salesperson).

The successful questioning to understand a customers goal, the further creation of a valuable solution by communicating the necessary information that encourages a buyer to achieve his goal at an economic cost is the responsibility of the sales person or the sales engine (e.g. internet, vending machine etc).

The primary function of professional sales is to generate and close leads, educate prospects, fill needs and satisfy wants of consumers appropriately, and therefore turn prospective customers into actual ones.

From a marketing point of view, selling is one of the methods of promotion used by marketers. Other promotional techniques include advertising, sales promotion, publicity, and public relations.

Various sales strategies exist, such as tit-for-tat which is best if ongoing dealings and interactions are expected. This insight is behind so-called consultative sales process which are used by Saturn to sell cars, as well as for some direct Business-to-Business sales.

Several types of sales exist including direct, consultative, and complex sales. Complex sales varies from other types in that thee customer plays a more pro-active role, often requiring proposal response to their Request for Proposal (RFP).

Psychotherapy

Psychotherapy is a set of techniques intended to cure or improve psychological and behavioral or emotional problems in humans. The commonest form of psychotherapy is direct personal contact between therapist and patient, mainly in the form of talking. Because sensitive topics are often discussed during psychotherapy, therapists are expected, and usually legally bound, to respect patient privacy and client confidentiality.

Psychoanalysis was the earliest form of psychotherapy, but many other theories and techniques are also now used by psychotherapists, psychologists, psychiatrists, personal growth facilitators and social workers. Techniques for group therapy have been developed.

While behaviour is often a target of the work, many approaches value working with feelings and thoughts. This is especially true of the psychodynamic schools of psychotherapy, which today include Jungian therapy and

Psychodrama as well as the psychoanalytic schools. Other approaches focus on the link between the mind and body and try to access deeper levels of the psyche through manipulation of the physical body. Examples are Rolfing, Pulsing and Postural Integration.

A distinction can also be made between those psychotherapies that employ a medical model and those that employ a humanistic model. In the medical model the client is seen as unwell and the therapist employs their skill to help them back to health. In the humanistic model the therapist facilitates learning in the individual and the clients own natural process draws them to a fuller understanding of themselves. An example would be Gestalt therapy.

Some psychodynamic practitioners distinguish between more uncovering and more supportive psychotherapy. Uncovering psychotherapy emphasizes facilitating clients' insight into the roots of their difficulties. The best-known example of an uncovering psychotherapy is classical psychoanalysis. Supportive psychotherapy, by contrast, stresses strengthening clients' defenses and often providing encouragement and advice. Depending on the client's personality, a more supportive or more uncovering approach may be optimal.

Cognitive behavioural therapy is particularly common where the mode of psychotherapy is dictated by the demands of insurance companies who wish to see a financially limited commitment. A computer program called ELIZA has been built to perform an automated and extremely simplified version of Rogerian psychotherapy.

There is considerable controversy over which form of psychotherpy is most effective, and more specifically, which types of therapy are optimal for treating which sorts of problems. Psychotherapy outcome research -in which the effectiveness of psychotherapy is measured by questionnaires given to patients before, during, and after treatment- has had difficulty distinguishing between the different types of therapy. All types of therapy show overall effectiveness, with none showing significantly better results than any of the others. Many psychotherapists believe that the nuances of psychotherapy cannot be captured by this type of research, and prefer to rely on their own clinical experiences and conceptual arguments to support the type of treatment they practice.

4

Intercultural Communication Principles

Intercultural communication principles guide the process of exchanging meaningful and unambiguous information across cultural boundaries in a way that preserves mutual respect and minimises antagonism. For these purposes, culture is a shared system of symbols, beliefs, attitudes, values, expectations, and norms of behaviour. It refers to coherent groups of people whether resident wholly or partly within state territories, or existing without residence in any particular territory. Hence, these principles may have equal relevance when a tourist seeks help, where two well-established independent corporations attempt to merge their operations, and where politicians attempt to negotiate world peace.

Methods for Communication and Culture

The Semiotics of Communication analyses the verbal and non-verbal codes used to transfer information between people. Should these people have different cultural backgrounds, they may interpret verbal and non-verbal signals differently. Empirical methods for researching such differences propose that culture is learned by listening to, and observing the behaviour of, other members within the group. Direct and indirect interactions ensure that culture is passed from person to person and from generation to generation.

The research methods are predominantly objective and quantitative, observing behaviour without considering the reasons behind it, and cataloguing the types of behavior identified as common within each culture. Data collection by observation is the primary method because intervention by the observer to ask for an explanation of the behaviour may produce unreliable subjective data and skew future behaviour when individuals are aware that they are being observed. But if researchers hypothesise that culture is coherent within the group because they share basic values (the assumption is that people think before they do), they must try to identify these basic values by inference or induction.

A soft systems approach would explore multi-causal explanations of behaviour. Complexity would be assumed given age, gender, ethnicity, religion, class, personality, reaction to authority, the setting, the other party's behavior, and the presence or absence of an audience. This approach allows for more nuanced explanations but it may produce detailed explanations that are more difficult to use as a predictive tool.

People from different cultures encode and decode messages differently, increasing the chances of misunderstanding, so the safety-first consequence of recognising cultural differences should be to assume that everyone's thoughts and actions are not just like ours. The main types of misunderstanding are:

Language

Even when two people think they can speak each other's language, the chance of error is high. Usages and contextual inferences may be completely different between cultures. So even though one speaker may have learned the vocabulary of the other's language, selecting the most appropriate words, with the correct intonation, spoken with appropriate eye contact while standing a proper distance from the other are all critical even before one considers the propriety of the topic to be discussed.

Rights, values, and Needs

Some cultural characteristics will be easy to identify, e.g. whether people are conscious of status or make displays of material wealth. But many rights are assumed, values are implied, and needs are unspoken, (e.g. for safety, security, love, a sense of belonging to a group, self-esteem, and the ability to attain one's goals).

For example, issues of personal security, dignity, and control will be very different as between an abled and a disabled person. Similarly, there may be problems of respect when a person from a rigidly class-based culture meets a meritocrat, or where there is racism, sexism or religious intolerance in play. In such situations, identity is fundamental when disputing the proper role or "place" of the other, about who is in control of their lives, and how they present themselves to the outside world. But the reality is more deeply rooted in power relationships: about who is on top of the social, economic, and/or political hierarchy.

Family members or long term rivals may be obsessed with their mutual competition. The relationships between racial or ethnic groups may be affected by economic jealousy. Nations may assert that their political systems are superior. Such conflicts are difficult to resolve because no-one wants to be the loser, and few are willing to share the winnings. Stereotyping can aggravate these problems and prevent people from realising that there is another way to interpret a situation, or that other groups may define their rights in a different way. Hence, what may appear just or fair to one group can often seem unjust to an opposing group.

People may misinterpret each other's motives. For example, one group may assume that they are simply exchanging information about what they believe, but the other believes that they are negotiating a change in beahaviour. This is most likely to arise when the parties are not completely honest with each other from the outset. Individuals may wish to protect their privacy, corporations may be concerned about industrial espionage, and politicians may be bound by requirements of secrecy in the national interest. Nevertheless, clarifying the purpose of the interaction is essential to eliminating confusion, particularly if vested interests are involved.

If time is not a factor and those interacting approach their meetings with good will and patience, effective communication is more likely. But, if the parties are under pressure (whether generated by external circumstances or internal needs), emotions may colour the exchange. Prejudice is a short-cut decision-making tool. In a crisis, fear and anger may trigger more aggressive tactics, particularly if the meeting is being staged under the gaze of the news media.

Improving Intercultural Communication

It is essential that people research the cultures and communication conventions of those whom they propose to meet. This will mininise the risk of making the elementary mistakes. It is also prudent to set a clear agenda so that everyone understands the nature and purpose of the interaction. When language skills are unequal, clarifying one's meaning in four ways will improve communication:

1. avoid using slang and idioms, choosing words that will convey only the most specific denotative meaning;
2. listen carefully and, if in doubt, ask for confirmation of understanding (particularly important if local accents and pronunciation are a problem);
3. recognise that accenting and intonation can cause meaning to vary significantly; and
4. respect the local communication formalities and styles, and watch for any changes in body language.

If it is not possible to learn the other's language, it is expedient to show some respect by learning a few words. In all important exchanges, a translator can convey the message. When writing, the choice of words represent the relationship between the reader and the writer so more thought and care should be invested in the text since it may well be thoroughly analysed by the recipient.

5

Nonverbal Communication

Most daily conversations are conducted face-to-face, the body playing a supporting role in communication. In many circumstances, people use emblems or gestures that can stand alone. Most of the time, however, humans communicate with one another by combining spoken language with body "language". Verbal and nonverbal communication are linked together synchronously, forming a complete presentation to the partipant or observer. This verbal and nonverbal interface must exist for humans to communicate fully. It is the body, however, that conveys most of the emotional semantics in communicative interactions.

The potential of human communication is realized only when body messages and spoken messages work together synchronously and harmoniously. Dysfunction and confusion result when the spoken word is contradicted by body messages. In face-to-face situations, the entire body is presented to the observer. In mediated situations, however, the body is masked. For example, when using e-mail, people substitute for emotions that are normally displayed in face-to-face situations by creating emoticons.

Emotional and paralinguistic cues are artificially produced by e-mail users. It is only in face-to-face communication that the full communicative reportoire can be expressed. In face-to-face situations, people reveal emotions and rhetorical sensitivity as they construct joint, intersubjective nonverbal messages. They can create healthy relationships or they can create dysfunctional relationships.

Nonverbal skills and competencies, of course, are learned. Some pathologies exist, such as autism or schizophrenia, which appear to be neuro-chemically induced; other body related diseases, such as anexoria or body dysmorphic disease appear to be the result of distorted perceptions. Pathologies, such as these, are displayed in particular ways, as in a frozen smile, a reptilian stare, or a very thin body. Normally, however, individuals learn how to use and display their bodies just as they learned how to use spoken and written language, yet a number of scholars indicate that spoken language and nonverbal behavior are processed in different ways in the brain.

People create a milieau and live within it; both the built and the natural environment are part of the context that influences human behavior. Artifacts, such as buildings, clothes and communicative technologies are created by humans; these artifacts influence their behaviors in turn. The social environment includes dyadic, group and public situations, such as ceremonies and rituals in which humans engage themselves. The built environment includes houses and public structures. Cultural thoughtways influence how buildings are structured. For example, Frank Lloyd Wright, a prominent American architect, designed homes that fit into the environment; the Navajo designed the hogan, a round-shaped building that grew out of their values, beliefs and practices.

Symbolic Interactionist Perspective

The Symbolic Interactionist perspective puts emphasis

upon human action, or agentry, and upon intersubjectivity and interpretation. People try to make sense of the nonverbal behavior of others and of themselves attaching meaning to the behaviors. Humans frame their worlds drawing upon their own personal experiences, their personal identity and life scripts. People respond to factual situations, to symbolic worlds found in literature, film, TV and books; they create meanings from what they observe others doing, in what they see themselves doing. They perceive, think, create lines of action, interact and then reflect upon the meaning of social events. The SI approach provides a way of looking at the naturally occuring world of human behavior.

All human beings create action sequences. They go to school; they drive a car; they read books; they go to movies, sing, play sports and so on. These action sequences have symbolic value, recognized as forms of doing. Sequences of action are made up of singular acts; for example, people know how to drive cars, but they learned, mastering one simple act, then another. In this process, drivers create schemes; they know the procedural rules, the techniques and so on. Given sufficient practice, they drive almost nonconsciously.

Sequences of acts are usually planned in inner conversations with the self. When performed often, they become routine, requiring little pre-thinking. They are symbolic activities. Drivers invest meaning in what they are doing and derive meaning from doing it. They can tell others what it means to get a driver's license; they can share their joy in being able to take a trip. Whether the action is a simple handshake or a complex display of elaborate rituals, actions such as driving a car, human acts always carry a symbolic mantle, either from the actor's view or from the observer's view. In this sense, the study of nonverbal communication is communication about human actions. The meanings of human actions are shared intersubjectively, forming the basis of community.

Symbolic interactionists suggest that the "actor" is always in the process of doing or thinking about doing; humans are influenced by others in interaction, in groups, institutions, society and culture. Society is not "out there"; rather humans engage interactively to produce society, engaging in self-talk, or conversations with themselves, to interpret behaviors. People take up multiple roles; indeed, they have many versions of themselves, not simply one, which are observed by themselves and others. People continually evaluate, negotiate, and produce "reality".

Nonverbal action is usually associated with verbal activity, although it can stand alone. It is dynamic and creative, but it may be patterned and somewhat predictable. Individuals may plan and create lines of action; on the other hand, they may act and react spontaneously. Although people are agentive on their own behalf, they are also interpreters of the actions of others. In short, they are performers and they are audience members. The human body is always present in social, interactive situations. When e-mail is used, humans construct self images as they relate to others who cannot see them.

Obviously, the human body is a physical entity, but it is the symbolic meaning that humans attach to the body that is important. For example, when people wish to make their bodies beautiful or handsome, they work on the images that their culture or society presents to them. People share cultural meanings associated with beauty which vary from culture to culture. In the United States, the media portray the images of beauty in ways that are endlessly clear to the viewer, whether the observer accepts the images or not. In short, the participant in social interaction must decide what to do with the "stuff" of society, to try to make sense of it.

Body Identity

The sense of a body self, or body identity is inevitably connected to a sense of the social self. The body of course is ever present, always communicating, intended or not. Humans inevitably must construct or create meanings for their bodies, by taking account of the meanings that are imbedded in society and culture. People are able to make quite accurate statements about themselves, about their own bodies, although they may at times deceive themselves. Statements about the self and the body are designed to fit the circumstances. For example, people create fictitious selves on the internet, describing themselves in ways that they hope may appeal to others.

People perceive themselves and others symbolically, labeling their own bodies and the bodies of others. People hold conversations with themselves, about themselves, about others and about events. In short, there is a symbolic, cognitive activity involved in the presentation of self and in the interpretation of the nonverbal behaviors of others.

In everyday life, humans create meanings by drawing upon implicit assumptions rooted in their personal life experiences; in professional research, on the other hand, scholars make their assumptions explicit so that they are testable and useful. There are several elements involved in human nonverbal communication. Cultural, social and psychological factors enter into nonverbal communication in complex ways, as do gender, ethnicity, age and technology. The milieu, or social contexts, influence human nonverbal communication because these themes are deeply embedded in the contexts of everyday life. Each of these themes contain hidden codes.

Space, time and the physical environment influence human nonverbal communication as well. These themes, or background factors, inevitably influence behavior because people take account of the social contexts in which they act. Meaningful lines of action are best created when people are aware of the dynamics of the social context in which they find themselves. Nonverbal communication is deeply influenced by these dynamic elements.

Humans are socialized into their worlds but, in becoming socialized, they take part in their own creative unfolding, not being passive; the baby gradually learns to use her body in appropriate ways. As humans go through life to a gerontological or even a centenarian age, they learn to construct new ways of thinking and doing, to modify their own identities, to alter the ways that they use the body. Humans enact strategies of behavior that will help them adapt and survive in a complex social world.

Nonverbal communication is a dynamic process that engages the mind, body and society as intersubjective entities. Humans create symbolic meanings for--and attach them to--the behaviors of self and others. They are influenced by the contexts of action and by master themes in society. In inner conversations with the self, or self-talk, humans propose and enact lines of action to fulfill the perceived demands of the situation, or the expectations of others. In this dramaturgy of behavior, humans learn to modify their nonverbal behaviors to meet the demands of new situations. Human identity, achieved in interaction, is poignantly expressed in self presentations.

Behavior and Communication

Distinctions between behavior and communication are often made by scholars who study nonverbal communication. For example, it is suggested that spoken words represent something symbolically, but nonverbal communication is not representative of anything else. It stands for itself. The better expression would be behavioral communication, the result of blending the concepts of behavior and communication. Except when people are talking within themselves, in self-talk, they are performing acts of meaning in interaction with others.

The interpretation of self behaviors and the interpretation of others' behaviors is essentially a subjective, symbolic process; that is, to interpret behaviors, whether it is of the self or of others, requires one to think in meaning terms, essentially linguistic in nature. That nonverbal behaviors may arise in different areas of the brain than does spoken language is not the issue. The end result is that people create meanings in interaction. Even when people perform acts that are not meant to convey meaning to others, observers take note of the behavior and interpret it as they see fit regardless of the inner workings of neuronal processes.

In short, people are always "on stage" being observed by others, unless, of course, they are simply ignored or dismissed. The communication-behavior nexus is firm and unavoidable; to focus only upon intentional nonverbal communication without stressing the "accidental" side is to miss what is going on in the theater of action. Humans act intersubjectively, sharing meaningful behaviors with fellow humans. Humans are inveterate actors and observers.

Differences Between Verbal and Nonverbal Communication

A number of scholars have delineated the differences between verbal and nonverbal communication, some suggesting that they are principally localized in different areas of the brain, the verbal in the left hemisphere and the nonverbal in the right hemisphere; that the verbal is primarily culturally based while the nonverbal is primarily biologically based; and that the verbal is digital while the nonverbal is analogic. Further, they are processed differently in the brain, the verbal being processed discretely while the nonverbal is processed as a gestalt.

Continued research refines the knowledge about human nonverbal communication. For example, it is suggested that spoken language is predicated on a kind of nonverbal corporeal semantics and that the intimate nature of bodily processes are inseparable from verbal processes. It is clear that some aspects of nonverbal behavior are lodged within the individual, unseen, while others are on display publicly. In self-talk, people make sense of events and they make plans or form intended lines of action. These acts of meaning, public and private, are part of the same sensemaking process.

Complexity of Nonverbal Communication

People seem to use their bodies almost effortlessly, almost routinely without thinking. But, of course, the effortlessness is due to their experience. Everyday routines are the result of learning and achievement. Once learned, some body behaviors are displayed in the same way again and again without the necessity of personal attention or awareness. Indeed, it would appear that many behaviors are mindlessly enacted. Research reveals that a complex web of factors influence an individual's behavior. The ability to manage and present oneself varies considerably in the general population due to a variety of hidden influences.

The complexity of human nonverbal communication may be illustrated by referring to research dealing with the physical face and the eyes, the face being the primary expresser of emotions, having features that seem to have minimum universality. The face displays primary emotions in unique ways. The study of oculesics, the pupils of the human eye, shows that they respond variously to different circumstances. The pupil either closes or widens under fearful or friendly conditions.

Eye movement is a key part of facial behavior, directing others' attention or showing surprise or happiness and other emotional displays. Eye gaze and gaze aversion help observers to know what the actor is up to. It is commonly believed that when people avoid looking one another in the eye that they are not trustworthy, or that they are lying. Are the eyes the window to the soul? Probably not. Cultural display rules influence how people use their faces and eyes. Black and Asian American children, for example, are taught not to look at an adult directly in the eye. Does this mean that they were lying? Stereotypes must be sorted out. The eyes are invariably involved in facial displays.

The face seems to emit emotionally contagious expressions; for example, a smiling face may prompt a spontaneous response in another person. Facial expressions show approval, encourage friendship or deceive others. Unfortunately most humans are not terribly good at detecting deception. The leakage hypothesis suggests that, in some Freudian way, the human body leaks information even when actors are not aware of it. Perceptive, trained observers can sometimes unmask these hidden meanings. There appears to be a public interest in unmasking the personae of others, ferreting out nonverbal leakage.

For example, professionals claim to be able to pick jurists by observing their nonverbal behaviors searching out those leaks of information that might indicate whether the potential juror is qualified to serve on the jury. Probably most people are interested in knowing the hidden secrets of others. In short, people try to make sense of how others use their eyes and their faces in interaction. The entire body, not just the eyes or face is involved in nonverbal communication.

Nonconscious Conmmunication

Nonconscious communication refers to the fact that humans act nonverbally without paying attention to themselves. People are not always aware of themselves. The word unconscious, used instead by some writers, may refer to persons who literally are not awake, as is said about the boxer who is knocked out. The use of the word nonconscious refers to the fact that people can be awake but unobserving or unaware of what is going on about them. Of course, human action may operate below the perceptual or sensory threshold. For example, research shows that the the face buzzes with activity hidden just below the visual threshold.

If it were necessary for humans to keep track of their breathing, the way they walk, or how they swing their arms, they would do little else in life. Habituated behavior enables people to get through the day without unnecessary attention to what they are doing. Dressing for the day, walking to school, having coffee and so on, tasks that may be simple or complex, can be performed without special attention.

Accidental and Intentional Nonverbal Communication

Unlike most other primates, humans plan to do things and then they bring them about. That is, they clothe themselves to keep warm or cool, but, depending on their outlook, they may also dress to show themselves off. In daily discourse, humans use their bodies to make a point, to emphasize or illustrate what they are saying. People can point a finger in an emblematic gesture and convey a definite meaning, no words required. In short, they send intentional messages.

Humans use strategies; they play games; they try to influence others using their bodies. When working jointly with others in common tasks, such as in playing in an orchestra, humans use their bodies in very specific skilled ways; otherwise, they cannot play the part. Humans perform meaningful and intentional acts in the presence of others.

But nonverbal presentations may be judged by others in ways that were not intended by the actor; unintended messages may be received and interpreted by observors. In these instances communication is accidental. In short, humans are always on stage whether they choose to be or not. People "shine" and give off signals and cues that they did not intend to send.

Signs, Symbols, Codes and Display Rules

Social semiotics is a science of language, both verbal and nonverbal. Semioticians make distinctions between signs, symbols, codes and display rules. A sign is denotative and specific. It points to something, as smoke may indicate a fire. A reddened face may indicate that the owner is embarrassed or weary from body exertion. The interpretation is usually framed in context. That is, when a young lady's face is reddened from physical exertion, one knows that she is not embarrassed. The context furnishes the clues to the meaning of her reddened face.

Signs and their usage vary from culture to culture. They are polysemic; that is, different persons may interpret them differently, there being many possible meanings. Signs, of course, occur in contexts which aid in their interpretation. Symbols tend to be more complex kinds of signs. Humans create symbols arbitrarily to represent things, people or events. Symbols may be non-specific but meaningful. For example, it is said that wine symbolizes romance, health and the good life. Similarly, a wedding ring symbolizes one's commitment to another; it symbolizes durable value and beauty.

Symbols may exist in a master form, as in the Mona Lisa or the Statue of Liberty but their symbolic value lies in their interpretation by the observor, who has a frame of reference. In short, master symbols are embedded deeply in a culture or society. Individuals born into that society must learn to make sense of the symbols. Humans construct society and cultural elements; in turn, they must learn how to manage in a cultural milieu that is loaded with symbols. As part of symbolic interactionism, humans learn about cultural symbols, they use symbolic language and they symbolize the human body. They make sense of things; they create meanings.

For example, the word mother may convey comfort, caring and attentiveness; the word father may convey strength, goal mastery and so on. To the abused child, the words mother and father may mean something very frightful. Interpretation, therefore, depends on contexts. Codes refer to broader categories than do signs or symbols. They are not fixed entities; rather, they are modified over time, in keeping with social change. Deeply buried within a given society are underlying codes that inform humans how they should behave.

For example, underlying codes indicate that people should shake hands or issue other forms of pleasant greetings when they first meet. Codes exist even though they may not be written down; humans learn about codes through indirect socialization, as they become aware of social expectations. Behaviors, habits and beliefs are shaped around these underlying codes or display rules.

Emblematic and Gestural Communication

Emblems are body acts that require no verbal accompaniment to be understood. Hand signals, such as waving goodbye, the V for victory sign, the high five signalling victory--all are examples of emblems. Nonverbal emblems may be sufficiently stable to categorize and label them. Scholars have constructed emblem dictionaries illustrating emblematic usage around the world. Not all people know the meanings of emblems just as they may not know the meanings of some words.

An emblematic sign in one culture may mean something quite different in another, as in the use of the zero shape made by the fingers, which in American culture refers to one thing but in some European societies means something else, perhaps embarrassingly so. Meaning "OK" in English it may be a "bad" expression in other cultures, something that is not OK. Thus an emblem may be a taboo expression. Pantomime is a special form of emblematic communication; few, if any, words are needed to convey what the pantomimist wants to convey.

Artifacts, Ceremonies and Rituals

Artifacts are used in human nonverbal communication, often in the background. The word objectics is sometimes used to refer to artifacts. A boat, a watch or perfumes are artifactual in that they tell observers something about their users. Artifacts are not simply lifeless physical objects; contrarily, people invest meaning in them. They are semantic indicators. Thus, a watch, purchased to tell time, may also convey the status or social standing of the owner to the observer. Artifacts may reveal to others the values of their owners. Archaeologists are specially trained to read artifacts, to show how they represented cultures from the past.

Ritualistic and ceremonial behaviors are usually collective events. Customs and holidays are celebrated by social gatherings, special foods, games and other activities. They reflect cultural values and folkways and they exist separately from the individual who takes part in them. Rituals are often associated with religious activities, although much everyday behavior can be ritualized. Rituals are social events, usually jointly performed, that are nonverbal in nature. Going to church, attending synagogue, going to the football game and so on can become ritualized, yet deeply imbued with meaning. They are recognizable, patterned activities that exist in all cultures in different forms.

Ceremonies, similar to rituals, are usually public events that are jointly produced. The wedding ceremony, the funeral, rites of passage, births and so on are ceremonialized according to social custom. For the individuals involved, they take on meaning according to the experiences, life construals and frames of references of the individuals involved. Ceremonies, rituals and artifactual usage occur in all societies, conveying deeply held meanings with which the individual must come to terms.

Ceremonial events may be quite structured although they may be altered from one generation to another; they may convey joy, bonding or togetherness, or enact or depict myths, depending on their function in society. Ceremonies involve life and death and all that falls in-between. They can act as rites of passage.

Human Sensorium and Related Phenomena

The Senses

Some texts about nonverbal communication include sections dealing with the sixth sense. However, there has been considerable debate by researchers over whether humans can and do communicate by using the sxith sense. The field of study, called parapsychology, has inspired research from both sides, from the skeptics to the believers, the so-called goats and sheep. People who claim to have extrasensorial abilities are fairly numerous in popular

American culture. Although there is good reason to discuss the sixth sense, given its place in the popular mind and in the minds of some scholars, there is far less clarity about parapsychological research than there is about the five senses; which, when taken together are referred to as the human sensorium, the five basic senses which all primates have.

Ethologists, those who study animal behaviors, usually from an evolutionary perspective, point out the sensate differences that are found among various species. Dogs, for example, have a well developed sense of smell; owls have well developed hearing and visual abilities; and monkeys and chimpanzees have well developed tactile abilities. All creatures have a neurological system; they are sentient, capable of sensing things in their environment. Evolutionists and ethologists emphasize that this differential development of the senses is due to the need for each species to adapt to complex environmental circumstances in order to survive. Thus, animals who hunt at night need good vision, for example.

Unlike most other primates, humans, who sit atop the primate evolutionary ladder, can knowingly improve the use of their senses. They can employ tools, develop their sensitivities, train the body, build muscles and so on, all of which seems to enable humans to take part in their own evolution. As an everyday example, the ordinary human may not be able to discern between the fine nuances and bouquets found in various wines, but the enologist, trained to do so, can detect and distinguish thousands of odors and tastes associated with wine. Indeed, chemists have created an elaborate vocabulary detailing very fine nuances of smells and tastes that is useful to specialist.

Although some lower order animals seem to create tools and make plans, it is not clear how much cognitive ability primates share with humans, although recent evidence suggests that chimps and humans are not far apart genetically.

Smell and taste are referred to as chemical senses. That is, they are very closely associated with each other and in close proximity to the brain, serving rudimentary functions. They are referred to as olfactory and gustatory processes. As in the case of tactility, or touch, they come into play mostly when they are in immediate contact with foods or other items. The chemical senses change as humans age; they are affected by hormonal changes in women who are menstruating or giving birth.

Smell and taste perform important basal functions, such as enhancing as food odors. In short, there are cultural overlays resting on top of the physical function of smelling. Another line of inquiry suggests that humans have individualized olfactory signatures. Pheromones, active in lower order animals in the sexual act, may be active in humans, influencing the mating, courtship ritual. Scientific research needs to validate the possibility. They have put a perfume on the market called Pheromone.

Humans can encourage affiliation or they can discourage contact, merely by how they use their eyes. There are cultural, gender and ethnic differences among humans influencing how they use their eyes and in how that use is interpreted by observers. Staring is a common nonverbal activity found among lower order animals. Aurality refers to the ability of humans to hear, an ability that varies highly among cultures. It also is age-related. The young enjoy loud music; the old enjoy softer music.

Hearing can be improve with training. For example, a recent study showed that conductors could hear orchestral sounds that others in the orchestra could not detect. However, the human hearing mechanism does not permit them to hear as well as many lower order animals. In some lower order animals, the use of echolocation mechanisms help them as they hunt, mate or move about in the physical environment.

Tactility, or haptics, refers to one's ability to touch and feel, the skin being the largest sensitive organ in the human body. Touching has been associated with gentling and bonding in both humans and other primates and to attitudes about body accessibility and self-confidence. The human skin is sufficiently sensitive that individuals can discern writing patterns performed on their backs, out of sight. The ability to touch, or grasp, differs among lower and higher order species; for example, it is clear that a hippopotamus cannot grasp a tree limb as a simian can. In the case of humans, the use of the fingers, thumbs and hands occurs within the field of vision, greatly enhancing human tactile abilities. Touching, holding, pushing, grasping, shaping, or throwing come easily to human beings. Humans take these activities and possibilities for granted. Most lower order animals can not perform these tasks.

Display rules suggest that how people touch one another conveys important and specific meanings. The question has been asked whether there is a right touch. There are power touches, professional touches, intimacy touches and so on, each having social codes attached. Laws protect citizens from inappropriate touch, as in rape or beatings. In short, touching must be acceptable and appropriate. At one extreme lies touch aversion; that is, some people fear the touch of others, based on their negative experiences. At the other extreme, there is supportive touch. It is said that some cultures promote touch starvation; that is, the natives seem to be starved for affection, which they may not get in interpersonal situations.

In sum, research about the five senses and how they interact in the daily lives of human beings is increasing. Research is showing how these sensory mechanisms, sometimes referred to as nonverbal channels, work together, how they are used in gendered ways, how they vary between cultures and ethnic groups and so on. It is obvious that humans need to know little about these mechanisms even though they rely on them for information. Research suggests that in the Western world especially, the eyes take primacy, not surprising in an age of television and film; nor is it surprising that engineers have created machines that hear, speak, listen, and send odors.

"Sixth" Sense

Returning to the topic of the sixth sense. Is there a sixth sense? Do people know things other than through use of the corporal senses? Considerable research has been conducted on human subjects, in an attempt to determine whether telepathy, aura reading, precognition, clairvoyance, remote viewing, the moving of objects by kinetic energy and other phenomena are legitimate aspects of human experience; if so, how are they to be interpreted? The field of parapsychology has serious scholars researching and working on the many issues involved. Again, many scholars dismiss entirely the claims of parapsychologists.

One major issue is whether results of experiments can be replicated; another major issue deals with the nature of the experimentation itself. Subjects, who are thought to have some telepathic ability, often called psychics or sensitives—terms that are often used pejoratively--complain that laboratory situations restrict their performances. For example, Ganzfeld experiments require the subject to be deprived sensorily by placing blinders over the eyes while the eyes are kept open. White noise is used as a mask throughout the experiment. The subject is asked to receive a message telepathically from the sender outside the cage while these sensory impediments are in place. This bizarre experimental method seems to be faulty on the face of it because subjects claim that it interferes with their psychic senses.

A third issue seems to be centered on the effect of belief. If one is a believer, perhaps she or he is more likely to claim that unusual experiences are psychic experiences. Research about psychic phenomena, the world of parapsychology, seems to be interesting to most people ; yet, the sixth sense does not seem to be established clearly enough to give it the sixth sense label. This is not to say that people who experience psychic phenomena are to be disregarded. Indeed, future research may reveal much more than is presently known. Perhaps new research paradigms will yield better results; the models used until now seem to fail.

Somatypes

Humans are fond of watching one another; the body, of course, is gendered. Women and men present themselves to others, whether their body action is confined to the eyes, the entire head, the trunk of the body or the entire body. Body behaviors have been given considerable attention in the research literature, as has somatyping, the idea that body shape and size are correlated with certain kinds of behaviors. Endomorphic, mesomorphic or ectomorphic shapes have been described. In early research it was believed that ectomorphs, the tall, thin people, had delicate personalities; medium sized people, the mesomorphs, were generally outgoing or athletic. The endomorphs, very heavy people, were thought to be languorous and slow.

Correlation is not causation, although it is often interpreted as causational. Biological structure may influence attitudes, but it does not predetermine attitudes; attitudes are created by the owner of the body, who in turn is influenced by her or his society. The importance of perceptions and stereotypes associated with body size and shape cannot be overstated, especially in Western countries, where body ideals are promoted by the media, a powerful force in Western societies.

Body Language

Body communication has been studied under the general name of kinesics. People often associate the idea of bodily communication exclusively with the use of gestures, but the field of study is now much broader. A body lexicon used to describe body behavior was created in early research including words like kines, morphs, kinemorphic constructions and other words, created to enhance the study of nonverbal behavior. A kine is the smallest unit of body expression, such as a facial movement; a morph may express the movement by two or more head motions; and, a kinemorphic construction may refer to the movement of the entire upper torso----all in synchrony with the verbal stream. Using this body language system, researchers have attempted to show how the verbal and the nonverbal streams work together in synchrony. Dancing, for example, reveals the integration of the body and how it manifests action signs.

Paralanguage

Semioticians focus on the ways that spoken language is tied into human behavior and they are able to differentiate between male and female language use. Within spoken language there are paralinguistic features. Paralinguistic studies focus on how humans use language, rather than with what they actually say. Emotional elements are expressed in everyday conversation; gender and social class markers are found there. For example, older people, males and females and members of various ethnic groups, use different voice pitch, loudness or range of tonality, compared to one another. Females typically have a higher vocal range than do males as is commonly observed. This difference, of course, is not absolute. To a large extent, it is a learned difference.

The word genderlect has been used to the distinctive ways that males and females express themselves, as learned through socialization. Not only do males and females differ in the patterning of vocal sounds, but they tend to use different sentence phrasing, different conversational styles and different conversational floor patterns, including different conversational turn-taking styles. Animated vocalization has been associated with extroverted personalities, while interrupted speech patterns have been associated with mental and emotional disturbance. Attempts have been made to associate psychological and personality traits with vocal patterns and various paralinguistic styles. As one can hear that the vocal patterns, or voice set, of older people, are very different from the vocal patterns of young children.

Environmental Influences

Proxemics

It is obvious that humans move about in space; less obvious, is that their ways of moving about vary considerably, based on the ways they have been socialized. Smaller in body, females need less space generally speaking than do males. The ways that the British, the Japanese, the Arabs and others from other areas of the world use space differ, sometimes substantially. Americans tend to feel crowded when people enter their personal space closer than three feet, the desired norm. Arabs, on the other hand, feel quite normal when they are close to one another in dyads or groups.

It has been said that the ways humans use space is governed by a hidden language; hidden codes exist, guiding people, although they are not aware of them. Humans become aware of the norms of space when that space has been violated. Spatial zones of interaction have been devised, varying by cultures. For example, intimate distance, personal distance, social distance and public distances vary considerably. The concept of zero proxemics implies that there is no space between bodies, a condition, which, in most instances, makes humans feel uncomfortable.

In loving situations, of course, one expects to be touching, body to body. A mother who does not touch her child is said to be cold and reserved. On the other hand, in other situations, space violations occur, as in rape, physical abuse and other demeaning activities. In general, extreme body closeness is shunned from culture to culture but there is considerable variation between cultures.

The concept of territoriality, a concept borrowed from the ethological study of animals, suggests strongly that humans, like other species, share normative expectations about how their space is claimed. Humans mark their spaces, perhaps by putting a purse on the table to define their space in their absence, or by putting fences between them and their neighbors. Lower order species, by contrast, mark their territory by urination or body rubbing.

When students enter classrooms, they tend to choose their seats in accordance with their perception of comfort, barring other reasons, as sociometrists have shown. The use of space varies enormously from situation to situation, from culture to culture; nevertheless, humans follow hidden display rules and context codes as they determine how they will use space.

Chronemics

Chronemics is the study of the human invention and use

of time. In some societies, it is clear that humans are almost cultish about time; they follow a cult of the clock. Researchers suggest that humans have built- in physiological, psychological and social clocks and that there are biological rhythms which vary according to age and sex. For example, some people work best in the morning while others work best at night, like sparrows and owls.

Time, of course, is a human conception. It does not have fixed dimensions. Early Native Americans relied upon seasonal changes for their sense of time, as do many members of traditional cultures in various parts of the globe. Today, some modern Navajo members may live away from the Reservation working in an industry that is governed by the hourly clock, returning at night to the Reservation, where different meanings for time are used.

The sense of time is related even to emotional and body health. Seasonal Affective Disorder (SAD), a form of depression, has been reported to be associated with the dark months of winter. Speed in walking, talking and behaving vary highly between and among regions of the United States based on the underlying hidden codes for the region.

Some cultures are past-oriented; others are present or future-oriented. It is said that American youth tend to be future-oriented while older citizens tend to be past oriented. These generalizations appear to have some validity; but, of course, humans are free to change the way they think and behave.

Environmental Influences on Nonverbal Communication

The environment influences nonverbal communication. Colors in the background are thought to influence moods and behaviors. For example, the soft color of green is often painted onto library walls furnishing a quiet, restful context. Bright red would seem to destroy the study mood. Unfortunately, the study of color and its influence on human behavior is only beginning to receive solid research attention. Anecdotal and popular notions seem to be pervasive. Yet, from a practical view, it seems that humans choose colors in clothing, in their houses, or for their cars because they like them or feel comfortable with them. Not just any color will work for them.

Humans don warm clothing in the winter and shed it in the summer. Clearly, humans create behaviors that are influenced by background variables. The physical environment, like the social environment, is a powerful influence on human behaviors, although the research is not substantial. Humans create architectural environments which reflect cultural values. As mentioned, the famous Frank Lloyd Wright designed houses to blend into the landscape, creating a prairie style. His houses were designed to let the outdoors in, by using large windows, subdued lighting, skylights and overhangs. Earthy colors were used to blend the buildings into the landscape. This great American architect influenced generations of later architects. He built his houses to fit into the environment, as no prior architect had done, showing Americans how to live more meaningfully within the environmental context.

On a less appealing side, American architecture, referring especially to public buildings, has been referred to as "hard architecture", meaning that it conforms little to comfortable human use, being designed for the faceless public person. Railroads, prisons, banks and other buildings are said to be hard, rather than soft, and to restrict rather than to open. Modern architecture and ergonomic development attempt to build better structures, more accommodating to the comfort of the users.

Architectural variations throughout the world reflect the values of their builders. The buildings of slash and burn cultures are necessarily temporary; the open courtyards of the Spanish built structures, found in South America and Spain, reflect the need for space, using courtyards. The tribal Navajo member had a sense of place and space that used open pastoral scenes, that incorporated traditional views of the four major directions, that oriented the natives to natural phenomena, such as the sun and the moon. Architectural structures and patterns arise from symbolic meaning of space, time and place found in each culture.

Human identity is rooted in the interpretation and perception of the self, a psychological activity. In interaction with others and in conversations with the self, humans create their identities. They learn that there is an I and a Me in the self and that both are observable in human action. The I is active; the Me is responsive, both being key parts of the sense of self and identity. Self concepts, identity and the construal of the meanings of human behavior is the work of psychologists, communicologists and others.

The concept of face is closely allied with the concept of identity. Not to be confused with the physical face, it is symbolic. Humans present themselves to others symbolically, using their bodies and their words. People learn how to save face or to promote a confident face. They learn to ingratiate themselves with others. The face gets construed and scripted. People learn to avoid embarrassment and to create positive impressions in the minds of others, who act as audiences.

Psychologists reveal that humans use action language, creating plans for action, both simple and omplex, to accomplish goals. They look back on their activities and make sense of them, building upon them, acting coordinatively with others in joint activities. They evaluate their own success or failure as they interact with others. A complex action may involve days, months or weeks of planned activity, such as those involved in courtships; or, they may be very simple, such as the brushing of the teeth in the morning. Each activity is meaningful to the participant.

A variety of communication models are used in the study of the general field of Communication and, more specifically, in the subfield called Nonverbal Communication. Each model, or approach, has advantages or disadvantages. For example, a sender-message-receiver model is popular in Communication, a linear view. This approach has been widely used in quantitative studies. The symbolic interactionist approach, has a number of advantages not shared by the SMR model, including the view that humans are creative, taking part in an interactive setting in special ways, not necessarily predictable.

Nonverbal communication is not a linear process. It is a contingent process; humans build one action upon another, reflecting upon what they have done in preparation for the next episode. They negotiate and modify their actions as needed.

Nonverbal Communication Research

Human, gendered identity is constructed and achieved; it is created in a long-term process, influenced by complex, often poorly understood elements in society. It is implied sometimes that identity, personality and character are fixed, unchanging concepts; contrarily, they are dynamic, yet fairly enduring clusters of focused concepts. Socialized from birth, humans choose, often unwittingly, how they will define themselves. Even though they are born with explicit sexual characteristics, they will genderize their identities.

Many scholars who hold an essentialist view of sex tend to show how males and females differ categorically; however, they fail to take into account that humans can and do define and redefine themselves as they choose, changing the ways they act in different circumstances. In saying this, it is not meant to imply that the creation of identity is a thoroughly rational process in which all of the elements are clearly known or depicted. Indeed, quite the opposite is often the case. Humans are often confused as they try to come to terms with self identification, especially in a society heavily saturated by the media.

There are biological differences that clearly influence gendered behavior; men do not give birth or have menstrual periods, although it is claimed by some researchers that men have their own pronounced biological shifts. Women in general have smaller bodies than do men. Even this comparative smallness is amenable to alteration. Women can and do become physically powerful. The concept of gender is a powerful, modern concept influencing nonverbal communication.

Ethnicity

Race and ethnicity are powerful themes in Western society; indeed, they are universal themes, meaning different things in different cultures. It is no accident that some cultures place people on the social class ladder based on their color alone. Like gender, concepts about race and color are learned. People are born into a colored world but they create the meanings of the world for themselves. Humans construe the meaning of skin color. In relatively simple and static societies, people know where they stand socially, based on skin color; in complex, change-oriented societies, people may move about in society and create new meanings about ethnicity, race or skin color.

Unfortunately, in the United States, a country that espouses an egalitarian ethos, where all people are to be treated equally, entire populations of colored persons have been—in many cases still are—treated as strangers by the dominant and prevailing white class, based almost entirely on the color of skin, although other factors come into play. This stranger-making process is complex and it varies according to the groups being studied.

Native Americans, or the Navajo, Black Americans and Chinese Americans are studied along the lines of how they achieved their identity in a white world. Identity is the key nonverbal concept and in the case of each of the above, the stuff of history has forced them to deal with their place in a white society. The presence of Cuban Americans in the United States arises from a very different social motif; usually, they have been treated as friends who fled a hostile home country to find a sense of place in the United States.

Idea of Ageism

The study of aging, as opposed to the idea of ageism, is about changes in the ways that humans symbolize themselves over a the lifetime. Although biological and genetic factors are influences on the aging processes, they do not determine aging in an absolute sense. Biology influences but does not determine how people age. Stage theorists emphasize the ways that humans are influenced at various stages in their lives. Stages are not fixed and individuals vary greatly among themselves in the ways that they age. Successful aging, a concept that is emerging in modern research, is described in positive ways.

Some aspects of aging do not seem to be under human control, such as the loss of acuity in vision, or the ability to see the color blue. Yet, with technological changes and new medical techniques, the shift from the deficit concepts associated with aging have changed to positive concepts about aging. Present day models of the aging process reveal that aging need not be deleterious! The new paradigms emphasize the role of the aging person, as an active, dynamic person, acting on his or her own behalf to sustain a successful life style.

Technology and Mediation

People in highly developed technical societies live in environments that are highly saturated by the media. Television in particular deeply influences members of these societies. Technological change is profoundly altering the social landscape of advanced countries.

New Media Environment

It appears that print and broadcast media are merging; that there is media abundance, rather than media scarcity. It is now possible to tailor media content to specific, targeted audiences. Interactive media is taking the place of one-way media. The Information Superhighway is controlled in the main by large corporations or businesses, who use it for their own purposes. At the same time, individuals can construct their own websites.

The internet appears to provide unlimited channels to communicate; it can be used to build communities, to create commerce and for a variety of activities that tend to blur the lines between providers and consumers. Mediation in modern societies is a powerful influence on nonverbal communication. The inventor of the internet referred to his invention as a world brain, indicating that the internet functions almost like a neurological net spanning the globe. Other technologies, such as the telephone, e-mail, television, movies and modern satellites have become so common in daily life that they form an embedded social web of which people are largely unconscious.

The new technologies are producing new, symbolic boundaries, new networked, global communities. Oral culture retains nonverbal, face-to-face situations, employing the full range of the human sensorium; but, as sophisticated communicative technologies emerge, the face-to-face character of oral culture disappears. In short, the technological context influences nonverbal communication, both in assumption and practice.

The computer and television have most dramatically altered the social landscape, with more than half of American households owning computers and more than ninety percent having television sets, many owning more than one. Embedded now in the social landscape, television and the computer have dramatically altered how humans perceive things and how they make sense of their worlds.

6

Communication Theory

Communication is a slippery concept, and while we may casually use the word with some frequency, it is difficult to arrive at a precise definition that is agreeable to most of those who consider themselves communication scholars. Communication is so deeply rooted in human behaviors and the structures of society that it is difficult to think of social or behavioral events that are absent communication.

Communication consists of transmitting information from one person to another. In fact, many scholars of communication take this as a working definition, and use Lasswell's maxim ("who says what to whom to what effect") as a means of circumscribing the field of communication. Some says that there is a ritual process of communication that cannot be artificially abstracted from a particular historical and social context. As a relatively young field of inquiry, it is probably premature to expect a conceptualization of communication that is shared among all or most of those who work in the area. Furthermore, communication theory itself is, in many ways, an attempt to describe and explain precisely what communication is.

Indeed, a theory is some form of explanation of a class of observed phenomena. Karl Popper colorfully described theory as "the net which we throw out in order to catch the world--to rationalize, explain, and dominate it." The idea of a theory lies at the heart of any scholarly process, and while those in the social sciences tend to adopt the tests of a good theory from the natural sciences, many who study communication adhere to an idea of theory that is akin to that found in other academic fields. Nonetheless, when evaluating the strength of a theory, the criteria commonly found in the sciences, and derived from the scientific method are often broadly applicable.

Evaluating Theory

Six criteria might be said to be properties of a strong theory. (The terminology presented here is drawn from Littlejohn, Theories of Human Communication, but a similar set of criteria are widely accepted both within and outside the field of communication.) In most cases, a theory that may only be applied within a fairly narrow set of circumstances is not considered as useful as a theory that encompasses a very wide range of communicative interactions. The ideal, of course, is a theory that succinctly explains the nature of human communication as a whole.

Theoretical Scope

In most cases, a theory that may only be applied within a fairly narrow set of circumstances is not considered as useful as a theory that encompasses a very wide range of communicative interactions. The ideal, of course, is a theory that succinctly explains the nature of human communication as a whole.

Appropriateness

Theories are often evaluated based upon how well their epistemological, ontological, and axiological assumptions relate to the issue or question being explained. If a theory recapitulates its assumptions (if it is tautological), it is not an effective theory.

Heuristic Value

Some theories suggest the ways in which further research may be conducted. By presenting an explanatory model, the theory generates questions or hypotheses that can be operationalized relatively easily. In practical terms, the success of a theory may rest on how readily other researchers may continue to do fruitful work in reaction or support.

Validity

It may seem obvious that for a theory to be good, it must also be valid. Validity refers to the degree to which the theory accurately represents the true state of the world. Are the arguments internally consistent and are its predictions and claims derived logically from its assumptions? Many also require that theories be falsifiable; that is, theories that present predictions that—if they prove to be incorrect—invalidate the theory. The absence of such questions significantly reduces the value of the theory, since a theory that cannot be proven false (perhaps) cannot be shown to be accurate, either.

Parsimony

The law of parsimony (Occam's razor) dictates that a theory should provide the simplest possible (viable) explanation for a phenomenon. Others suggest that good theory exhibits an aesthetic quality, that a good theory is beautiful or natural. That it leads to an "Aha!" moment in which an explanation feels as if it fits.

Openness

Theories, perhaps paradoxically, should not exist to the absolute exclusion of other theories. Theory should not be dogma: it should encourage and provide both for skepticism and should--to whatever degree possible—be compatible with other accepted theory.

It is important to note that a theory is not "true," or "false" (despite the above discussion of falsifiability), but rather better or worse at explaining the causes of a particular event. Especially within the social sciences, we may find several different theories that each explain a phenomenon in useful ways. There is value in being able to use theories as "lenses" through which you can understand communication, and through which you can understand the world together with other scholars.

Theories and Models

A simple communication model with a sender which transfers a message containing information to a receiver. Many suggest that there is no such thing as a successful body of communication theory, but that we have been relatively more successful in generating models of communication. A model, according to a seminal 1952 article by Karl Deutsch ("On Communication Models in the Social Sciences"), is "a structure of symbols and operating rules which is supposed to match a set of relevant points in an existing structure or process." In other words, it is a simplified representation or template of a process that can be used to help understand the nature of communication in a social setting. Such models are necessarily not one-to-one maps of the real world, but they are successful only insofar as they accurately represent the most important elements of the real world, and the dynamics of their relationship to one another.

Deutsch suggests that a model should provide four functions. It should organize a complex system (while being as general as possible), and should provide an heuristic function. Both these functions are similar to those listed above for theories. He goes on to suggest models should be as original as possible, that they should not be obvious enough that they fail to shed light on the existing system. They should also provide some form of measurement of the system that will work analogously within the model and within the actual system being observed.

Models are tools of inquiry in a way that theories may not be. By representing the system being observed, they provide a way of working through the problems of a "real world" system in a more abstract way. As such, they lend themselves to the eventual construction of theory, though it may be that theory of the sort found in the natural sciences is something that cannot be achieved in the social sciences. Unfortunately, while models provide the "what" and the "how," they are not as suited to explaining "why," and therefore are rarely as satisfying as strong theory.

Laws and Rules

The aim in the natural sciences is to create what, since Hempel at least, has been called covering law. Covering law requires the explicit relationship of a causal condition to an effect within certain bounderies. It has been observed that social relationships are very difficult to capture within the structure of covering law. Perhaps this is because people have the annoying habit of violating "natural laws." Wittgenstein's later work in particular put forward the possibility that rules-based systems may provide a more effective descriptive model of human communication. This may account for the propensity of communication theorists to develop models more often than theory. Rules-based approaches are particularly popular within speech communication, where human interaction is seen to proceed along structural, though not necessarily causal, lines.

Theoretical Landscape

A discipline is defined in large part by its theoretical structure. Instead communication, at its present state, might be considered a field of inquiry. Theory is often borrowed from other social sciences, while communication provides few examples of theories that have been exported to other disciplines. What is taught as communication theory at one institution is unlikely to be at all similar to what is taught within other communication schools.

This theoretical variegation makes it difficult to come to terms with the field as a whole. That said, there are some common taxonomies that are used to divide up the range of communication research. Two common mappings will be briefly presented here. Many authors and researchers divide communication by what are sometimes called "contexts" or "levels," but more often represent institutional histories. The study of communication in the US, while occurring within departments of psychology, sociology, linguistics, and anthropology among others, generally developed from schools of rhetoric and schools of journalism.

While many of these have become "departments of communication," they often retain their historical roots, adhering largely to theories from speech communication in the former case, and mass media in the latter. The great divide between speech communication and mass communication is joined by a number of smaller sub-areas of communication research, including intercultural and international communication, small group communication,

communication technology, policy and legal studies of communication, telecommunication, and work done under a variety of other labels. Some of these departments take a largely social science perspective, others tend more heavily toward the humanities, and still others are geared more toward production and professional preparation.

These "levels" of communication provide some way of grouping communication theories, but inevitably, there are theories and concepts that leak from one area to another, or that fail to find a home at all. If communication is a cohesive field of study, one would expect to see a cohesive set of theories, or at least a common understanding of the structure of the field, and this appears to still be developing.

Another way of dividing up the communication field emphasizes the assumptions that undergird particular theories, models, and approaches. While this tends also to be based on institutional divisions, theories within each of the seven "traditions" of communication theory that Robert Craig suggests tend to reinforce one another, and retain the same ground epistemological and axiological assumptions. His traditions include the rhetorical, semiotic, phenomenological, cybernetic, sociopsychological, and sociocultural traditions. Each of these are, for Craig, clearly defined against the others and remain cohesive approaches to describing communicative behavior. As a taxonomic aid, these labels help to organize theory by its assumptions, and help researchers to understand the reasons some theories may be incommensurable.

While these two approaches are very commony used, it seems that they decentralize the place of language and machines as communicative technologies. The idea that communication is the primary tool of a species that is defined by its tools remains at the outskirts of communication theory. It is represented somewhat in the Toronto School of communication theory (alternatively sometimes called medium theory) as represented by the work of Innis, McLuhan, and others. It seems that the ways in which individuals and groups use the technologies of communication—and in some cases are used by them—remains central to what communication researchers do, and the ideas that surround this, and in particular the place of persuasion, are constants across both the "traditions" and "levels" of communication theory.

7

Theory of Symbolic Interactionism

Symbolic Interactionism is a theoretical approach to understanding the relationship between humans and society. The basic notion of symbolic interactionism is that human action and interaction are understandable only through the exchange of meaningful communication or symbols. In this approach, humans are portrayed as acting as opposed to being acted upon. The main principles of symbolic interactionism as outlined by Blumer (1986) are:

1. human beings act toward things on the basis of the meanings that things have for them
2. these meanings arise of out of social interaction
3. social action results from a fitting together of individual lines of action

This approach stands in contrast to the strict behaviorism of psychological theories prevalent at the time it was first formulated (in the 1920s and 1930s), behaviorism and ethology, and also contrasts with structural-functionalism. According to Symbolic Interactionism, humans are distinct from infrahumans (lower animals) because infrahumans simply respond to their environment (i.e., a stimulus evokes a response or stimulus -> response) whereas humans have the ability to interrupt that process (i.e., stimulus -> cognition -> response). Additionally, infrahumans are unable to conceive of alternative responses to gestures. Humans, however, can. This understanding should not be taken to indicate that humans never behave in a strict stimulus -> response fashion, but rather that humans have the capability of not responding in that fashion (and do so much of the time). This perspective is also rooted in phenomenological thought (see social constructionism and phenomonology.

According to symbolic interactionism, the objective world has no reality for humans, only subjectively-defined objects have meaning. Meanings are not entities that are bestowed on humans and learned by habituation. Instead, meanings can be altered through the creative capabilities of humans, and individuals may influence the many meanings that form their society. Human society, therefore, is a social product. It should also be noted that symbolic interactionists advocate a particular methodology. Because they see meaning as the fundamental component of human/society interaction, studying human/society interaction requires getting at that meaning. Thus, symbolic interactionists tend to employ more qualitative rather than quantitative methods in their research.

Additional Concepts

Society

In symbolic interactionist thought, there is a difference between infrahuman and human society. In infrahuman life, cooperation is physiologically determined. In other words, it is not a cognitive process; it results from instinct and biological programming rather than conscious thinking. In human society, cooperation is cognitive and conscious. Human cooperation can only be brought about by:

— each acting individual ascertaining the intention of the acts of others

— each acting individual deciding on his/her own response on the basis of that intention

Another distinction drawn between infrahumans and humans is in the types of communication employed. Infrahuman communication is gestural; it takes place immediately, without any interruption of the act for interpretation or assigning meaning. In contrast to infrahuman communication, human communication is meaningful in that gestures are symbolic and do not invoke immediate responses - humans must interpret gestures and assign them meaning. Because human communication involves interpretation and the assignment of meaning, it is only possible when there is consensus in meaning. Meanings for symbols must be shared. Shared meaning necessarily takes place through role-taking; in order to complete an act, the actor must put himself in the position of the other person. Behavior is viewed as social not simply when it is a response to others, but rather when it has incorporated in it the behavior of others. Human beings respond to themselves as other persons respond to them, and in so doing they imaginatively share the conduct of others.

Self

The self refers to the conscious, reflective personality of an individual. It is the entity the person envisions when he/she thinks about who they are. In order to understand the concept of self, it is important to understand that the development of self is only possible through role-taking. In order to look upon your self, you have to be able to take the role of another, which, in turn, allows you to reflect upon your self. Because role-taking is a necessary part of self-development, it is concurrent with the development of self. According to Mead, the self develops in a series of three stages:

1. *preparatory stage* : meaningless imitation by the infant
2. *play stage* : actual playing of roles occurs; but no unified conception of self develops
3. *game stage* : this is the completion stage of self-development; the child finds who he or she is; the child also must respond to simultaneous roles; the individual can act with a certain amount of consistency in a variety of situations because he/she acts in accordance with a generalized set of expectations and definitions he/she has internalized

The self consists of two parts, the I and the Me. The I is the impulsive tendency of the individual (similar to Freud's notion of the Id). The I is the spontaneous, unorganized aspect of human existence. The Me is the incorporated other (see generalized other) within the individual. The incorporated or generalized other supplies an organized set of attides and definitions, understandings and expectations (or meanings) that are common to the group to which the individual belongs (similar to Freud's concept of the superego).

According to Mead's presentation of the I and the Me, action begins in the form of the I and ends in the form of the Me; the I gives propulsion while the Me gives direction. Additionally, the I, being creative and spontaneous, provides for change in society. The Me, being regulatory, works to maintain society. Thus, in the concept of self is a powerful and comprehensive understanding of how humans function in society and, in turn, how society functions (by both changing and remaining constant). The concept also depicts the relationship between the individual and society.

According to Meltzer, there are three implications of selfhood:

1. the posession of self makes of the individual a society in miniature; humans can engage themselves in interaction; they can view themselves in a new way
2. the ability to act toward oneself makes possible an inner experience which need not reach overt expression; humans can have a mental life
3. an individual with a self can direct and control his behavior

It is also important to recognize that the self and the mind are twin emergents in the social process.

Mind

The Mind or mental component of man emerges out of human communication. The mind is only present when significant symbols (as opposed to gestures that do not have meaning but simply evoke responses) are being used in communication. In this sense, mind is a process manifested whenever the individual is interacting with himself using significant symbols (symbols or gestures with interpretations or meanings). The mind is also the component of the individual that interrupts responses to stimuli. It is the mind that attempts to pre-vision the future by exploring possible outcomes of actions before proceeding with actions. In minded behavior, the individual carries on an internal conversation.

8

Symbolic Interaction and Nonverbal Communication

Symbolic integration is a perspective that can enrich a researcher's analysis of human behavior and it can provide a way for the student to integrate studies in nonverbal communication; indeed, it can help a student frame and interpret nonverbal events. Researchers in various disciplines employ widely ranging models or paradigmsin their focus on human behavior. A research program may be very restrictive or it may be very broad, depending on the goals of the researcher. It may be confined to the laboratory or it may focus on the natural life-worlds of the subjects.

Major Concepts of Symbolic Integration (SI)

A vocabulary associated with SI has been developed over a long period of years. Major concepts include the following.

I

the proactive part of self, enactive and agentive.

Me

the sensitive, reflexive, more durable part of the self.

Self

a combination of I and Me in Meadian theory, created through interactions. The self is seen as a symbolic object.

Play

social activities in which children take part but which are microcosms of later social life.

Sensemaking

the interpretive activity of creating meaning of self, others and interactive behaviors

Role-taking

the ability to put onself in the place of another; intersubjective and shared understandings are the result.

Symbol

the semantic representation of the object's in one's life, whether they are physical, psychological or social. The building blocks of meaning.

Mind

a dynamic, socially oriented, behavioral and processual entity that enables humans to make sense of behavior and act accordingly.

Agentry

the ability of humans to enact lines of action on their own behalf to adapt to social circumstances.

Joint production of meaning

refers to the fact that humans cooperate and participate in actions, creating new social relations.

Frames of reference

perceptual lenses based on personal experiences that help people interpret human behaviors.

HUMAN BODY SYMBOLIZATION

The human body, of course, is involved in nearly all communicative episodes. Contrary to a common assumption, the body is not merely a flesh object with skin and bones. Rather, it has symbolic meaning to the owners and to others who observe it. In reflective conversations with themselves, people create meanings for their bodies as part of the way they experience the world. People evaluate their bodies, thinking of them as ugly or pretty, obese or thin. Psychological, social and cultural meanings are applied to the body. People incorporate the perceived attitudes of others in their self assessments.

The presentation of self is an everyday occurence and the body is intimately involved in these presentations. People learn how to use their bodies to influence others and to respond to them. As self presenters they are actors on a metaphorical stage; as observers of others, they are part of a metaphorical audience.

Self-concept

The self-concept is essentially the product of social interaction. The self is inescapably a social self. People create their identities based on the influence of others; parental and peer influence are of paramount importance.

Self, or identity, is expressed in verbal and nonverbal communication as a form of facework.

The self is involved in all nonverbal communication; lines of action are formed, based on the sense of self, and adapted to social circumstances. People perform multiple roles in life, such as lover, parent, child or worker. People perceive how to act appropriately to avoid personal embarrassment. They can misread situations and botch them; they can deceive others or "ham" it up. They can play simple or elaborate games to impress others, acting with considerable skill. They can also be very awkard and shy in the presence of others.

Human nonverbal communication is interactive and intersubjective; that is, there must be a sharing of meaning between participants in a nonverbal event for there to be mutual understanding. Display rules and codes are embedded in the social contexts of action; the concept of appropriateness is derived from the underlying codes. From one perspective, humans seem to play elaborate games in their interactions.

Social status influences human nonverbal behavior. For example, wealthy people born to money and to the associations and privileges of wealth, behave differently from those who are born in poverty, their codes of conduct having been derived from different contexts or standpoints in society. Their presentations of self reflect the status of the economically privileged person; the expectations of their peers reinforces their behavior. By acting as they are expected to, people of privilege consciously and unconsciously reinforce the norms of their social status, class or standing. Powerful master themes, such as social class, power and dominance, age, gender and ethnicity are involved in, and expressed through, everyday interactions. Humans create a sense of identity, which are really the sum of the ways that they think of themselves.

SI Nonverbal Process

Nonverbal behaviors are usually contingent, one behavior leading to the next. Most of the time, people are involved in social events where only two or a few more people are involved. Personal forms of agentry are typical. Many times, however, people are involved in large public and mass events, such as sports or musical events. Forms of public ritual are expressed in these circumstances. Whether they are marriage ceremonies, funerals, political conventions, or worship rituals, public events contain the social rules of engagement.

Intentional Nonverbal Communication

Perhaps most personal lines of action are preplanned and intentional, although the planning may be fuzzy or awkward. For example, people plan to dress fashionably for job interviews to make a good impression. They may even practice the interview in a dress rehearsal at home. On the other hand, many body behaviors are adaptive actions that require little previous thought. Scratching and itching are automatic responses to the signals that are sent by the central nervous system. People usually brush their teeth while thinking about other things, such as last night's date. Even when waving goodbye, the action is nearly phatic because people do it without deep meaning or thought. Routinized behaviors are habituated and often highly skilled, the result of considerable practice. Although they require little conscious attention, they are the products of learning.

Whether or not people intend to communicate something with their bodies, they are always on stage, either frontstage or backstage in one way or another. For example, people reading books in a library may be thoroughly engrossed in what they are doing, completely unaware that others may be observing them; their posture and so on, trying to make sense of who they are, attributing meanings to them. The reader has communicated something to the observer without intending to, completely unaware. In this sense, people are always on stage. Humans cannot not communicate. It is common for researchers to separate intentional and accidental communication, but both occur together.

Even when nonverbal communication is intended, as in the wink of an eye, the targeted observer may miss the connection altogether, focusing on something else. The separation of intentional and accidental communication by researchers helps them do their researcher, but it is artificial. There are levels and types of nonverbal communication. There may be singular episodes that are not repeated or there may be very complex, long-term behaviors. A rough form of planning is necessary to create a relationship, for example. Romantic relationships, seemingly simple, are indeed complex. They are contingent, recursive, non-linear involvements full of social and cultural meaning, deeply involving the emotions and personal schemas of the participants. Although the planning and staging of romantic involvements may be blurry, even confused, it is a necessary part of the romantic "spiral".

There are many short-term routines associated with maintaining a relationship, such as putting a piece of toast in the oven, or taking the other party out to lunch, but the overall relationships is exceptionally complex. People may "work" on nonverbal communication in self-talk or conversations with the self and never take any subsequent action. In other words, people can plan to do nothing that is observable to others, which, of course, is a often a chosen line of action. People may respond to perceived emergencies in signal response; they may also choose beforehand not to respond in the middle of the night to an accident involving others.

Nonverbal communication has been studied in various ways, from a variety of perspectives from very early times to the present. Roman orators taught their pupils how to speak; how to use their bodies in spoken presentation. Historiographers have shown us how queens and emperors lived and anthropologists have shown us cave paintings depicting nonverbal activities. Modern psychologists, philosophers and others have pieced together new approaches to the study of communication, as any book on nonverbal communication will reveal.

Everyday language rests on a nonverbal base. Children at birth rely on nonverbal means of communication, developing spoken language only later. The history of collective human growth reflects the same dependency of language upon a nonverbal base. Space, time, custom and practice; the ways that humans think about themselves and adorn themselves; and the ways they paint, use artifacts and construct buildings---all of these activities find their way into the spoken language.

Symbols

The human language is symbolic; that is, people create metaphors for their bodies and for the events in their life-worlds. Symbols are arbitraily constructed by people and they become short-cuts to meaning, used again and again. Symbols do not have meaning in themselves; humans attach meaning to them. For example, the Statue of Liberty is a symbol of freedom to many people; but others may find meaning in the fact that the statue is a woman. People invest meaning into objects, people and social situations. Symbols are a type of logic-in-use, passed on from one generation to the next. The white dove has symbolized peace and freedom for centuries. Symbols may be shared publicly, but they often have private, individualized meanings. Each person uses the symbol in specially construed ways.

Body Symbolization

Unlike lower order animals, humans have the ability to "see" their bodies, which become objects of existence. They make sense of their bodies and label them using terms such as beautiful, ugly, obese or slim. Cultural and social meanings for the body are invested in the ways that people symbolize their bodies. Peers, fellow workers and parents bring their own sets of meanings to the person who reflects upon her body.

In a media-saturated society, images are played up; individuals take note of them and use them in their own self-evaluations. People know what a female "perfect 10" is and they know what a male "hunk" is. In other parts of the world the American body index may have little meaning because people construe the shape and form of the body in very different ways. Beauty in other countries may include the perception that large busts or bottoms are attractive to men, suggesting that the perception of attractiveness is a function of evolutionary development..

The body, a corpus of flesh, is socially defined. Humans think of themselves as young, middle age or old, as Black, Cuban, Navajo or Chinese, as male or female. Each set of self labels is a learned, adapted perception. They are umbrella terms that help people adapt socially. Group members are conscious of an identity, although it may be loosely constructed and quite general. The labels may be applied rigidly or flexibly. But the point is, they are invented as part of the self identification process.

Symbols are somewhat stable, especially in cultures that are slow to change; they are transportable from generation to generation. Even colors have meanings that are associated with different cultures. Red, for example, is particularly important to the Chinese. The legal profession in America uses royal blue and purple colors as part of its distinctive history. Each individual attaches meaning to colors, preferring one over the other.

Signs and Icons

Signs, symbols and icons have been extensively studied by semioticians. They believe that signs and human action are bound together. They are studied as tools that give meaning to everyday life. Symbols are a class of signs as are icons. While a sign designates something—for example, the classic smoke therefore fire process—an icon represents an entity often by bearing likeness. The importance of signs, symbols and icons to human action can not be overestimated. Indeed, if they did not exist the normal processes in society would disappear. Traffic lights and road signs, but one simple example, regulate the flow patterns of traffic. In addition, they represent the law of the land. In short, there is a critical relationship between signs and human behaviors. People who fear spiders or snakes or other things often react in frightened ways in signal response.

Icons may be very popular, such as the image of Elvis Presley who is said to be an American icon. Each generation, of course, creates its chosen icons. There is an inherent, inseparable relationship between signs, symbols and icons. They are tools that humans use to give meaning to their worlds. Cultures symbolize gender, age, or ethnicity in many different ways.

Cultural Symbols

Symbols are often unique to cultures. On the other hand, some symbols are known across cultures but given a slight twist of meaning by a particular culture. For example, in the Western world, the dragon has been symbolized as evil, part of the forces of evil. In the Eastern world, particularly in traditional China, the dragon is a symbol of joy, of dynamism and good health and fertility; it is a protector against evil. Sand is a symbol of purity in the Middle East, used even for washing, but, in the Western world, it is often thought of as an unstable element, impermanent, as in sinking sand. The Navajo tribal people have long used sand in artwork and in religious ceremonies. Thus symbol construction varies from culture to culture .

Human Interaction

SI scholars focus on interactive units of analysis and upon the theme of personal agentry; that is, humans are not caused to act, they act out of choice. They do, however, act in accordance with their interpretation of the demands of the situation. Their past experiences influence how they will act, but they act in the present drawing upon their past construals.

Although human behavior is patterned, it is not completely predictable. People can maintain situations, modify them, or ignore them completely. They can act alone or they can choose to join others in a joint action, even a cause. Humans, of course, are socialized in general ways. They create and maintain a sense of place, of context and situation. Feral children are not socialized and they cannot create a sense of place in an established society. In the final analysis, society is the collective result of all human actions. Society takes.on broad characteristics that distinguish it from others. One characteristic of democratic American society is that it promotes the egalitarian ethos.

Although humans become conscious of their bodies very early in life, they are not always conscious of the processes that influence them. People are often very attentive to needs, to self and to body; on the other hand, many people seem unaware of elementary aspects of life, such as emotions. In short, there are levels of awareness.

Many people are highly reflective; others seem to walk about unaware of self and others.

Self Identification

Self identification is a key to human growth; it is also a key to human interaction. People hold mini-theories about life, they have tacit knowledge about social matters; they have cognitive schemas that are based on their experiences from the past. Part of the self-labelling process results in a sense of self, labeled the symbolic face. People, of course, have a physical face, but the reference here is to the images that they present to others. The concept of face is psychological, social and cultural. The so-called frozen face of the Navajo or the Korean is physical, but the underlying cultural rules and norms are symbolic, It is said that American females exhibit a politeness bias because they "wear" a smile. The physical face is invariably entertwined with the symbolic face.

Face is related to role-playing; indeed, people create a professional face, such as that of a lawyer, a doctor or a plumber. The lines they enact are usually related to the notion of face. For example, the image of the doctor is maintained by her ability to perform medical procedures and to the fact that she has medical knowledge. Her lines of action are clearly representative of the profession. When they are not, she may, in fact, suffer the consequences. Professions require that their members maintain face. All humans, of course, have a symbolic face; it gets played out in identifiable ways, a type of symbolic signature.

Dramaturgy, or the acting component of human behavior is closely associated with impression management. The concept of first impressions is well-known. In short, humans present themselves, manage themselves in human interaction from a variety of postures, for a variety of reasons. Impression management may be skillful or awkward. As mentioned, shy people are frequently unskilled at interaction, withdrawing from it, even finding reasons for their behaviors. Thespians are trained to act in front of audiences and they are frequently skillful in daily interactions.

Actors and actresses have historically received voice training stemming from the early Romans and Greeks who knew the value of vocal power and robustness. The voice is a key part of human presentation and its paralinguistic qualities "give the person away". In short, humans try to perform in front of audiences, although they are differentially skilled at it. Many people, of course, are unaware that they are performing.

Context and Codes

Human behavior is always situated in time, place and space. It is situated in social context, a fact that deeply influences how human behavior is conducted. Social codes and display rules influence how people will behave. Nowhere written down, they are picked up on, caught during the socialization process. For example, young children learn not to burp in public. In this example, the parent may have directly socialized the child by giving it specific direction; on the other hand, the child may have learned how to behave indirectly, tacitly, by watching others. Either way, the implication is that the parent responds to socially imbedded codes that influence human conduct.

Such codes may be pandemic, across entire cultures, or they may be shared distinctively by certain members of society. What one should do on a foxhunt to identify with other foxhunters is a very specific example of hidden codes, associated with a sport that has traditionally been part of the ways that the wealthy in Britain live. Human experience is framed by coded information.

When human behavior is common to a society, it is considered normative, although it can be functional or dysfunctional. That is, not all behavior exhibited by large numbers of people are considered desirable, as in crime or hate group behaviors. People are put into prisons, a place where their freedoms are curtailed because of their negative behaviors. Prisons are total institutions that restrict and control behaviors.

Television presents framed sequences of human behavior that are recognized by the viewer. It has been suggested that television reflects human society, representing it and that it maintains the ongoing structural nature of society. This has been disputed by scholars, there being a wide number of research models dealing with television. However, television clearly frames human action, whatever the perspective, and it, too, must operate within contextual rules.

Compatible Approaches and Orientations

Joint Activity

Jerome Bruner and others have focused on joint or mutual knowledge and action. Humans bring to relationships verbal and nonverbal knowledge, which they share jointly. A child, watching her mother, takes part nonverbally in jointly attentive activities, such as mutual smiling, grasping and pointing. The mother and child sharing are intersubjective partners, as are other people who jointly act together. Reciprocity is based on correctly perceived intentions.

Action Theory

Human actions are always open to identification, whether an individual is identifying his own action or those of others. Identification is necessary so that people can understand one another. People hold implicit theories about how their actions will be received or understood. All plans have antecedent conditions; that is, one must have some kind of prior reason in order to act. Plans, images, scripts, intentions and goals arise from implicit theories. From this view, human behavior is what people think it is.

A common sense psychology pervades the way that people decide the meanings behind human activities; they seem to have a sense of the subconscious, of motivating factors and so on. In identifying meanings of acts, observers must make a connection, decide the intent, reflect upon it and attribute meaning to it. The stream of bodily action is accompanied by a stream of verbal action.

Mediated Self Theory

Modern American society is heavily saturated by the media, principally television and the internet. The effect of mediation upon human identity is the thrust of this work.

Semiotics

Semiotics is the study of meaning as expressed in signs, the smallest element of meaning. A symbol is a type of sign. Codes are sets of signs and rules. Assumptions about signs and codes lead to human action. Two people, from similar backgrounds, share in coded meanings. Anything can be a sign. For example, people see the behavior of others as signs. Codes are included in all human affairs, from science to art, from meditation to action. Symbols, types of signs, are polysemic; that is, they can be interpreted in multiple ways.

Impression Management

Theories, implicit and explicit, guide everyday human behavior. Whether people are driving their cars, playing golf or making love, they are engaged in the act of impression management. The presence of other people presents a possible stage of action. People act before others to influence them or to enhance their own self-images. The presentation of self is nearly always designed to achieve a goal.

Not all people are skilled at impression management, or self-presentation. Shy people, as mentioned, appear to lack the social skills to manage themselves well. Pathological conditions, of course, intrude upon the ability to present oneself successfully. Most people, however, can intentionally improve their abilities at impression management.

Ethology

Ethologists are usually persuaded by evolutionary theory; they may study humans or they may study lower order animals, such as primates. The behavior of animals can shed light on human behavior, as many ethologists have shown. At the same time, scientific ethology can uncover some of the mysteries of animal behaviors. They have shown, for example, that dolphins and chimps appear to have a sense of self, recognizing themselves in mirrors. They have shown that chimps can learn and use a nonverbal 'language' and they can use tools for their own purposes. Some researchers suggest that the differences between human behaviors and chimp behaviors is a matter of degree rather than kind, an issue that has been in the forefront of research for many years.

Postmodernism

Postmodernist research and writers bring a special

perspective to the meaning of symbolic life. They note that the social and cultural milieu found in modern, technologically advanced cultures is very different from that of industrial, or modern society. Humans, they say, now live in a post-modern age in which the authority structures are changing and the texts, or contexts of experience, are being decidedly modified. Relationships of power and dominance, of social class and ethnicity, of aging and gender, are being redefined.

Standpoint and co-cultures are two important terms related to self-identification processes. In a broad sense, women and people of color are achieving new vocalities, having new choices and the possibilities of redefinition of the circumstances in which they find themselves. The authority of institutions is diminishing, ushering in new possibilities for self-identification. New information technologies are leading to new ways to organize society. New social texts are being formed. Nonverbal communication will be influenced accordingly.

9

Cultural Influence on Nonverbal Communication

Culture is a cognitively symboled system, meaning that cultural interaction is based on a system of symbols and signs which the natives of that culture share. There are cultural "logics", every culture having a unique sense of semiosis. Humans are born into culture, they maintain it and pass it on to their children. Their lifeworlds are formed though the joint production of meaning . Humans interact symbolically, one with the other, acting out their lives in cultural spheres, such as the kinship group, clan or tribe. Knowledge, norms and symbols are passed from older generation to younger generation along with modes of work and play. Nonverbal behaviors are passed on as well.

Acculturation, or the processes involved in the acquiring of culture, influence human perceptions, which in turn, influence nonverbal behaviors and their interpretation. Cultures have permeable boundaries; they are not fixed. Variability in cultural patterning is obvious as are the contrasts between cultures. Being raised in China is very different from being raised in the United States, say, in St. Louis. The differences in linguistic habits, in customs and beliefs and in the daily patterns of life are clear to those who have spent time in both places. Yet, despite the differences, people living in both cultures are sufficiently similar, so that they share commonly in the tasks of living, growing and dying.

Television, film and digital culture, originally confined to Western countries, are now universally dispersed. Indeed, countries as different, one from the other, as Japan and the Netherlands belong to a new technology-based culture, a Northern belt, crossing the traditional boundaries of nation and cultures. As the popular saying implies, humans seem to be constructing a "global village". Could the multimedia explosion be leading to a "global mind" as well? Telematic networks are abolishing time and space which bear upon human identity.

Traditional cultures still exist and they provide contrasting examples of nonverbal communication. In nonverbal communication, nature meets culture.

Symbolic interactionism provides a way to view and understand human nonverbal communication. It is a dynamic, creative process that focuses on the symbolic meaning of human interaction. Humans construct meaning in their lives; they enact lines of nonverbal action and performance, as they try to adjust to and influence the people and events in their everyday lives. Not only do humans act in small groups they also engage in unique cultural and ceremonial practices with large numbers of people.

Readers need to be cautioned that not all members of a given culture think or think or act alike. Within any broad culture, there are ethnic groups whose ways of life separate them out from the mainline culture. Individuals, too, vary in the ways that they present themselves. The word culture is employed as a broad brush, lumping sometimes isolated groups together without giving explicit attention to the thought processes of each individual.

Scholars in the humanities and in the social sciences have shared mutual interests in culture over a period of several years; the boundaries between them appear to be disappearing. The way that culture is defined is often the result of the orientation of the individual researcher.

Multiple Interpretations

The word culture has many meanings. Popular culture, for example, deals with expressive forms which are spread widely throughout a society, often associated with mass communications. People decide what book to read, what film to watch or what social event to attend. High culture, or hoch kultur, on the other hand, is a term that is used to refer to a special or preferred set of social activities enjoyed by the few. For example, in the United States people who love opera are usually interested in other fine arts as well.

The perception is that classical music, museum art and archaeological activities are enjoyed by well educated and monied people. Popular culture, on the other hand, is usually associated with mass communication, film, radio, books and television. Despite these perceptual differences, given the powerful role of the mass media, the classical lively arts seem to be blending with popular culture forming a new cultural hybrid. By typing the word culture into a search engine on the internet, one may find more than fifty definitions and examples of culture, ranging from cyberculture to teenager culture. These uses of the word are specialized, applying to unique groups, associated with specialized activities.

A broader interpretion of culture is used in this text referring to all of the activities that comprise a person's life, including values, beliefs, habits, thoughtways, customs, technology, art, language, religion and ways of making a living. The word enculturation suggests that a person who is raised in a specific culture will exhibit the norms of that culture. In short, people are bathed in culture, completely immersed in it. As mentioned, the idea of culture may be unique to humans. Nevertheless, ethologists who study primate behavior including gorillas and chimps, the closest associates of humans on the evolutionary ladder, point to genetic and social similarities between higher primates and human beings.

For example, chimp genes may be useful in the prediction of disease patterns in humans, their genetic patterns being very similar to those of human beings. Research shows that chimps can use sign languages and even teach their offspring how to do the same. Perhaps chimps have a culture; chimps can use Ameslan and Yerkish, two nonverbal languages, to "talk" to humans and to one another. Whether chimps or other species have a culture or not is an interesting scientific puzzle; the meaning of the word culture is confined to its application to human beings in this book, although, at various points, ethological research is used for illustrative purposes.

Assimilation and Accommodation

Cultures may be impressed on people both formally and informally. For example, the Zuni of new Mexico have a formal culture that puts pressure on its members, which they cannot disregard if they are to remain members. Most Americans, on the other hand, are generally informal about their culture, except where serious tradition plays a strong role, emphasizing what is right and correct to do, as in fundamentalist religions.

Cultural Myths

Myths are forms of spiritual metaphor which help members of cultures organize rituals, celebrations and other human activities. There is a thematic quality to myths, such as stories about creation, heroic accounts, human quests, destructive floods and astronomical figures. Myths define cultures; they may be used to compare cultures. All cultures have myths that are passed on from generation to generation. The bee hunters, located in remote areas of India, for example, believe that the bee trees are benevolent females. This myth is passed on from parent to child; unfortunately, the tribe is diminishing in size as members die off. Eventually, the myth associated with the tree will disappear.

It has been argued that Eastern myths differ from Western myths in the ways that they allude to ultimate reality. In Eastern religions, myths are guides to the beyond. In the West, myths are often associated with icons, figurines or other representations, in the present. In the West, the Creator is involved in His creation.

Myths, of course, provide cultural meaning to the lives of everyday persons. Myths suggest that everyday life is natural or meant to be the way it is. But, analysis of cultural behavior reveals that culture is the product of human action heavily influenced by environmental factors, such as the presence of modern technologies. For example, past-oriented cultures have a degree of permanence that technologically oriented cultures do not have which gives rise to the belief that things are meant to be the way they are.

By comparison, one can actually observe changes taking place in technologically developed countries; the sense of permanency is lost. Grandparents in the United States tell their grandchildren about important changes over the span of their lifetime, from the rumble seat to the picture tube and the internet. Indeed, the speed of change is itself increasing. Communicative technologies are changing society in remarkable ways. The speed of change is faster in highly technical societies than it is in past-oriented, oral societies. For this reason, technologically advanced societies tend to be present or future oriented while societies that have relatively undeveloped technologies tend to be past-oriented. The achievement of identity is complicated in complex, modern societies. The routes to achievement become blurred.

Values are embedded in all cultures; as a child becomes enculturated, values are centered in the individual personality and reflected in behaviors. For example, if a society values openness and emotional expressiveness, individuals will reflect those values behaviorally in interaction with others. Values are guides to actions. The cultural background influences the individual; the individual's personal agentry and presentation of self reflect the expectations of others. If, for example, a culture permits the open display of emotions, its members will tend to freely display their emotions.

When people assimilate the culture they explore it proactively, adapting it to their needs. When people accommodate themselves to the culture, they adapt or accept, with little modification, the elements of culture and allow them to shape their thinking. Both verbal and nonverbal communicative behaviors reflect these processes. For example, the child raised in a Bedouin society, as a member of a wandering desert tribe, will learn to eat only with the right hand, following the ways of the elders in his tribe. Chinese in traditional China eat with chopsticks.

Cultural Dimensions

Cultures and the societies within them have been described in different ways by different scholars. For example, cultures are said to be high-context or low-context referring to how people in those cultures communicate. Members of high culture context tend to rely less on the written word, many of the meanings of their lives being hidden and unexpressed. Their cultural codes are more implicit than explicit, known by the individual but not expressed directly.

Traditional Japan is a high context society while the United States is a low context society. It is said about visitors to Japan, that although they may have mastered the language, they can not become fully saturated in Japanese culture because they were not born into it. They will always be outsiders. Cultures vary along an individualism-collectivism dimension, meaning that members in a highly individualist society, for example, will display individualistic behaviors, as in the United States. A Confucian saying applying to Chinese society, a collectivistic society, warns "If a nail sticks up, hammer it down." The ideas behind rugged individualism, demonstrated in the Western expansion movements in early America, do not apply to the Chinese.

Other dimensions that scholars emphasize include the uncertainty-avoidance continuum, the masculinity-feminity continuum, and the power-distance continuum. The word continuum implies that there is a range along which cultures vary, each culture being positioned at some point along that range. For example, people in highly male dominated societies, or patriarchies, as in parts of Latin America, may demonstrate a machismo attitude. The Cuban society, discussed in this book, reflects a system of machismo. Matriarchal societies, or those that reflect the emphasis upon the primacy of females, are found in parts of Africa and in past cultures where female goddesses were exhibited and worshipped. Power orientations are different, comparatively, in male and female oriented cultures.

The rugged individualistic tradition, so much a part of early American society, placed men above women in social affairs. Historically, the concept of rugged individualism applied mostly to males, a fact that influences gendered behaviors even in the modern world. The frontier spirit, the rough life, the male drive for gold in the mid-1800's emphasized male primacy, as part of rugged individualism. Levi jeans were built for the wear and tear of the male lifestyle. Today, of course, in a more relaxed society, females wear jeans; the male domination, so characteristic of earlier times, although not completely eroded, has been muted or moderated.

It may be tempting to oversimplify the characterization of cultures along the lines of one dimension or the other. In reality, the themes mentioned above are simplified ways of looking at the dynamics of any society or culture. Cultures are complex. Individual members display diverse behaviors. It is only by sustained, intimate exposure, by the immersion of oneself in a culture, that one can really understand that culture and appreciate the complexity and diversity of cultural life.

Both verbal and nonverbal communication form the base of culture. Humans develop a sense of the self, a cultural identity, that includes perceptions of the body and daily experiences. As social beings, humans engage in collective activities. The body becomes specially symbolized in every culture depending on cultural traditions. For example, in a popular vein in the United States, it is not uncommon to hear the human body described using a continuum from one to ten. The perfect body is a 10, hardly a universal concept.

Cultures vary comparatively, but there are rough resemblances of behavior in societies that share the same general culture. For example, the spoken language is a defining feature of all cultures; highly diversified, there are more than 2500 languages spoken, of which 82 are used by 96 percent of the population of the earth, most of which are unwritten. Nonverbal communication is highly varied, as well. The spoken language acts as a cultural lens, shaping and influencing human perceptions, while nonverbal communication is the action component. The two, acting together, reflect cultural norms.

Very early anthropological studies were conducted from a Western, European point of view. The research reflected the values of white male Europeans and Americans. This Western value orientation may be reflected in the concept of a hierarchy of races, a scheme based on the uses of the human body. This view suggested that the eye-man occupied the top of the hierarchy, characterized by Westerners; the ear-man came next, characterized by Asians; then followed the nose-man, represented by Native Americans, followed by the tongue-man, as found among the Australian aborigines. Finally, at the bottom of the hierarchy was the skin-man, as found among Africans. Doubtless, this scheme is errant and without merit; as mentioned, it reflected the values of early Western anthropologists. All senses, of course, are present in all cultures, although members of various cultures may appear to value one sense over another.

Using Symbols

Humans create meaning by using symbols to represent everyday life. Objects, events, humans, indeed all things, are symbolized by humans in the sensemaking process. As mentioned, the human body is presented in multiple ways in various cultures, ranging from colored bodies, as in the painted black bodies of ancient Mayans who associated black with evil and the underworld or the Blue Men who live among the Tuareg of the Sahara, so named for the color of dye that rubs onto the skin from their clothing.

The use of facial masks is an historic art form in China. Long hair was a symbol of manly strength, as in the Samson and Delilah story. The body is used even to convey class consciousness, as in the early Indian caste system where the human head represented the highest classes and the feet represented the outcastes. Goddesses and gods in early Greek and Roman times bore male and female images. In America, of course, the body is adorned, painted and colored to make one beautiful. In short, the body is the ultimate symbol.

Rituals associated with birth and death and all that is in between depict the body in various ways. The practices associated with birth and death vary highly between cultures as do rites of passage, such as firewalking. Common in various parts of the world, firewalking is used as a test of mind and spirit over matter. Painful flagellations, ear punctures or other forms of body infliction, are used in rites of passage to enable young males and females to pass into adulthood. Culture, ritual, place and pain are wound together in the practice of flagellation.

Both human and animal bodies are displayed in tourist places, as in postcards and other advertisements, and in zoos throughout the world as a form of staged tourism. Public displays of corporeality reveal identity, gender, ethnicity and culture. Not only do people watch people but they are fascinated by the behaviors of other species, especially the behavior of animals like pandas and chimps. In some countries where primates originate, they are often accorded mystical bonds with humans; in other countries, people are sometimes annoyed at the evolutionary association of humans with primates.

Self and Identity

Self and identity are associated concepts. Humans are uniquely able to take themselves as the object of their own thoughts. The ability to reflect on the self has deep implications for human behavior. For example, personal identity is often equated with ethnicity, which may be a concept applied to an individual or to a group. Identity may be conceived of as an unchanging fixed entity; however, it is a fluid concept. For example, one might say he is an American, from the American culture; yet, he would have to define it further, perhaps by indicating that he is a child of Swedish immigrants who migrated to Minnesota. In short, the meaning of identity is a loose construction, somewhat mythicised.

One's self identity is acculturated, which means that one acquires identity nonconsciously, not quite knowing how it happened. One gains a general semantic memory without having a specific episodic memory. Identity is achieved but one may not be aware of the events and processes associated with the achievement.

Cultural Production of Face

It has been said that nonverbal communication is where nature meets culture. Biological and social aspects of behavior are brought together in nonverbal communication. An important concept is that of "face". The concept of face is symbolic and it involves how individuals think of thmselves. It refers not only to the physical face, but to the symbolic aspects of self-presentation. The symbolic face is part and parcel of identity. Psycho-socio-cultural processes are imbedded in the concept of face.

To have face is to have self-respect. In Chinese culture, for example, mien-tzu refers to both a psychological and a social meaning of face, one that is conferred upon a deserving individual. In China, people are concerned most with their place in the scheme of things, their interconnectedness, following Confucian ideals. Thus the sense of self, of face, in China is very different from that found in the United States where a strong sense of personal independence is fostered. In

Japan, the word kao may refer to the personal body, to personal psychology ot to social behavior. In short, the concept of face implies self-presentation. Because cultures have different display rules for self-presentation, misunderstandings can arise when persons are not informed about the norms of the culture they are visiting. For example, gift giving is an important activity in both North Amerian and Asian cultures. An American might open a gift immediately but the Chinese person would be embarrassed or affronted, feeling a loss of face, were she required to open the gift immediately.

The physical face of course is part of human anatomy. Considerable research has been conducted dealing with the face and how it expresses emotions, referring to the facial primacy hypothesis. Everyday sense tells us that when people frown, grimace or smile they mean something by it. Exactly what they mean is not always clear. People may mask their feelings with a smile; they may play act with a frown; they may grimace but not be in pain. The frozen smile of many Native Americans or various Asian groups is worn in public, masking the inner thought-world and feelings of the individual. In brief, the information in body kinetics is open to interpretation. People may interpret human gestures stereotypically or they may interpret them polysemically. A smile can mean different things to different people.

Cultural Influences on the Senses

There may be a tendency for people to think of the senses as physiological mechanisms only, but the use of the senses, like the use of the face, is influenced by cultural meaning. Cultural values are expressed though the senses. Sensory symbolism refers to a social process. Were the readers of this book to travel to countries with contrasting historical and cultural backgrounds, they would note differences among cultures in the ways that they emphasize the senses—seeing, hearing, smelling, tasting or touching. For example, in oral cultures where there is little print or television influence there is less emphasis upon the specific use of the eyes relative to the other senses than is found in the United States where "the educated eye", so to speak, is emphasized.

Odors and smells vary radically from country to country illustrating the cultural habits and values of the country involved. Tactility and proximal closeness are valued differently by different countries and cultures. The English do not touch one another in public, nearly as much as do the Puerto Ricans, for example. People experience the world through their senses, but their senses are heavily influenced by cultural norms.

People even dream about sensate things. In experiments, thirty-three percent of men and forty percent of women in the United States could recall having senses of taste or smell in their dreams. Auditory scenes occurred in approximately 53 percent of all dreams reported. Smell and taste sensations were reported in only 1% of the dreams. It has been said that Americans hide and repress body odors, covering their bodies with perfumes. There is a blandness and sameness in American culture when it comes to body odors, according to this point of view. One ethnic group may claim that members of another group are identifiable by their body odors, as though individual members had body odor signatures.

The human ability to smell is not keen, at least when compared to the abilities of many lower order animals, such as dogs. Ethologists and animal communicologists show that nocturnal monkeys have a better sense of smell than do diurnal, or day monkeys Many animals, of course, use smells to mark their territories. This marking ability is less obvious in humans, although it seems to occur.

People may be identified by the perfume odors that they wear, which is a matter of choice. Not a matter of choice are the body odors that are emitted from the skin; pheromone research may reveal how the human body emits barely detectable odors. Perhaps the role of human pheromones will become clear as research continues.

In the United States, touching activity varies by gender, by place in society and by empowerment. A touching orientation is more commonly associated witih females than it is with males. Social touch has been related to social competence by some researchers. Interestingly, it has been said that Americans suffer from tactile deprivation noted, especially, in the situation in which a mother, herself deprived of a healthy attachment style during early childhood, fails to bond with her child through gentle touch. The power of gentling and bonding has been amply demonstrated not only in human studies but in studies or lower order primates. Grooming, licking and nudging are intimate ways to help lower order animals raise their offspring. Healthy human attachment and growth depend on the caring touch as well. Indeed, childhood psychotherapists speak of attachment disorders that afflict young children who have not been cared for in loving, tactile ways.

Influences on the Emotions

The study of the emotions has received considerable attention because they invariably accompany both verbal and nonverbal expression. The spoken language reveals emotional affect. The primacy of the face in showing emotions has been noted. Research suggests that emotional expressions as shown by the face have minimum universality; that is, various cultures share in common some features of emotional expression although they may interpret emotional expressions variously. For example, a smile is used by members of all cultures; however, the meaning of the smile is interpreted by taking account of the display rules in that culture.

A smile may be used to mask hidden feelings and people can create a facial display without having a corresponding emotion. Indeed, it has been suggested that females in many cultures tend to exhibit a politeness bias, using a smile to do so. The argument about the universality of both language and emotions has continued over the past few years. Six emotions, known in all cultures, have been studied fairly intensively. They are surprise, fear, disgust, anger, happiness and sadness. Sometimes the emotion labeled interest is added, resulting in the acronym SADFISH. When surprise is shown in these studies, the brows are raised, the eyelids are opened wide and the white of the eye shows more than it does when the eyes are in a resting position.

Facial blending, or the interaction of the eyes with the rest of the face is common, resulting in perceived anger or disgust, for example. Attempts have been made to see if members of different cultures perceive the displayed emotions in the same way. It appears, however, that there is minimal universality. That is, members of different cultures will view the emotions in different ways due to enculturation. Some emotions are easier to interpret than are others. Studies reveal that subjects are better at detecting happiness than they are at detecting disgust, for example. Perhaps they are better at displaying certain emotions as well.

Framing Emotions

Researchers have shown how emotional signals are used adaptively and when they are formed in a child's life. For example, distress signals are displayed at birth, the baby emerging into a booming, buzzing world of confusion. The social smile is displayed between 8 and 10 months of age;

joy is shown by the age of 5-7 months. In short, childhood growth is patterned.(Bruner, 1990) These behaviors may vary from culture to culture. Emotions are revealed in culture-specific ways. Again, it must be emphasized that humans slowly and gradually learn how to take account of the social influences found in their cultures; they make sense of those influences and develop lines of action accordingly. They learn how to present themselves appropriately in a variety of contexts.

Influences on Body Language, Posture and Gesture

The human body mediates all reflection and action upon the world and it has often been the subject of topics dealing with reproduction, the emotions, human sexuality and shamanism. It is assumed that culture provides the necessary labels for biological and behavioral acts. Cultural symbols for the body vary from culture to culture. The human body has been somatyped in various ways. Action theorists explain that there is a mind-body connection; actions are tied into antecedent thoughts. Mind, self and interacton are inherently bound together. People often make careful plans and then follow them after which they are able to explain what they have done. Following the SI approach, humans make sense of what they are doing. Their lines of action are often carefully crafted, even though, at times, humans seem to be on automatic pilot, doing even complicated things, apparently without thinking or planning. Researchers refer to body actions as kinesics.

The term kinesics is often translated as body language, body idiom or gesture language, each suggesting the intimately connected nature of gestures and kinesics. Posture is the key element in kinesics. Gestures are usually localized involving only the face, the upper torso or the hands and fingers. Emblems, unlike much kinesic behavior, can stand alone, without verbal accompaniment.

The shaking of hands, a ritual in many cultures, may be done without words being spoken; yet people know what it means. Cultural patterns are revealed in greeting rituals varying considerably from country to country. The Russian bear hug, the Eskimo nose rub, the arm grasp and the handshake are greeting patterns that are assumed to be the norm in each culture in which they are used. It is important to note that people are not required to know the origin of their greeting habits in order to use them efficiently and effectively. People present themselves to others using simple handshakes, gestures or gazes.

Body presentational practices vary widely between cultures. For example, women in the United States are taught to keep their legs together, unless they are wearing jeans, while men cross their legs. Inheriting the Judeo-Christian tradition, young Americans learn the place of modesty, although they may choose to ignore the underlying assumptions. Traditional Asian cultures require women to walk behind men. In India, women whose husbands died, were expected to be burned on the same funeral pyre with their dead husbands. This extreme practice, called suttee in India, is now disallowed, but it revealed the values and practices associated with some classes in India.

Hidden cultural display rules are obviously powerful; members must make sense of these display rules and incorporate them or risk being shunned or even banned in some circumstances. Indeed, shunning, or the banning of members for failing to fulfill the expectations of the social group of which they are members, is not an uncommon practice, even in the United States. Marrying an English, a reference to people outside their faith, is forbidden among conservative Amish groups. By marrying outside the faith and practices of the Amish, a person risks losing Amish identity. As mentioned, some cultural groups impress upon their members very clearly what is expected of them. Other groups are loosely knit, permitting a variety of behavioral patterns.

Twenty key gestures, including actions such as the fingertip kiss, the head toss and the thumps up gestures, were analyzed in 25 different countries, within 40 different contexts, involving 15 different languages. Showing pictographs, researchers asked the 1200 research subjects what each pictograph meant to them. The results showed that natives in neighboring countries often shared similar interpretations of the gestures while more remote natives varied in their interpretations. Distance was a key factor. The authors concluded that prejudice and religious beliefs, incorporated in language, influenced the gestural meanings. For example, where it is forbidden to display explicit sexual gestures, it may also be forbidden to display a simple finger kiss. The display rules in various cultures signal what is appropriate and what is taboo. A very large array of nonverbal gestures have been categorized and sorted out; the result is that a dictionary of emblems is available to the researcher or reader.

Body language complements verbal language in a synchronous manner. When humans speak vocally, their bodies "speak" nonvocally. As a topic shifts, the body may shift; even the vocal pattern changes at the end of a sentence. Eye use is correlated with the flow of speech as well. A person may look away or down, when she ends a sentence. In short, the senses and the body parts work together in human interaction, blending in a reportoire of bodily action. The eyes, however, have primacy in interaction.

Although people learn how to use their eyes in interaction, learning it from their parents and peers, even congenitally blind speakers use their eyes despite their lack of visual models. Further, it has been shown that babies born blind smile just as do their sighted peers. In fact, they apparently use body gestures structured like sentences and words. Therefore, a nature-nurture controversy exists, as to the sociobiological origin of gestures. Continued research will ferret out the relationships between what comes "naturally" and what is learned.

Meanwhile, it seems clear that context affects the use of gestures. Symbolic interactionism emphasizes the creative nature of human communication; humans must take into account the social influences of context, but they act on their own behalf, creatively. For example, it is considered inappropriate for young Japanese children to look their elders directly in the eyes.

Cultural Symbols

Symbols are cultural products. They are short-cuts to meaning. Created by humans, they take on a life of their own, existently independently of individuals. Symbols represent cultural beliefs, customs and practices. They exist "out there", enduring over time. Human language is symbolic; the human body is symbolized. Even human tools become symbolic; the hammer is associated with the carpenter; books are associated with people in academia, and so on. Symbols are carriers of coded information providing meaning to the individuals who use them. The computer is a tool that provides and organizes information; it also symbolizes a level of understanding to its users.

Symbols may be iconic and they may signal things. Elvis Presley, is to many, an American icon. The Statue of Liberty is a symbol of hope to many; it is visually iconic, sending meaningful signals to people who immigrate to the United States. Symbols are indicators of the aspirations, belief systems and neuroses of the cultures that generate them. Thus, the cross has come to signify Christian cultures; the Swastika, once an honored symbol in India, became a hideous symbol used by Hitler. All cultures have symbols, such as flags, to help identify and unite the members of that society. In short, people respond to symbols, as a form of signal response.

Humans create symbols and they become part of cultural transmission. Many of them are master symbols; that is, they. enjoy special status among people. For example, the cat became a powerful symbol in early Egypt after it rid the granaries of mice and rats. The cat was gradually elevated to mythical, symbolic status. Modern symbols are exported in the diffusion of innovation process. The logos of modern, powerful companies are exported around the globe, influencing various cultures. People may think of Nestles or Hersheys when they think about chocolate, the association having been made so clear by those chocolate companies. People who live outside that influence, of course, do not recognize the symbols. Inhabitants of the deep forests of New Guinea know less about Western symbols that do the French, for example. Their vocabulary does not include names for symbols with which they are unfamiliar. Yet, some symbols are known throughout the world. The author bought a Coca-Cola from a small boy at the top of a pyramid in the heart of the Guatemalan jungle. Vegetarian hamburgers are sold by MacDonald's in India.

Iconography is a field of study devoted to the study of visual symbols. An icon is a symbolic image. They exist in all cultures, some sacred, and others secular. The minnarets of the Muslim faith are recognized throughout the Muslim world, as are the veils worn by women. Words, too, can be iconic. For example, Superman comics contained the words "zow" and "kerplat" to indicate the physical prowess of Superman. Computer literate people know what an emoticon is but the young man driving the Amish horse-drawn carriage may know little about them. Context, once again, is important in human communication. It is suggested that members of highly developed technological societies are in the midst of an icon revolution, given the fast pace of change.

Symbols, Beliefs and Behaviors

Symbols need not be physical objects or icons. Activities, relationships, events, gestures and ritualistic activities are symbolic, too. People make symbolic sense of these activities. Symbols and their uses change over time. One point of view suggests that dominant American symbols once associated with religion or faith, both considered vertical dimensions, are now replaced by symbols that are rooted in a mass culture. The stock market, for example, is conceived from this point of view as a bottomline activity. The God(s) of the rural farmer are not those of the modern businessman, the assumption goes. The plow, not a product of mass culture, has given over to the computer and television, both mass products.

In pre-technical oral societies the NBC peacock is not known, but the symbols and rites of the shaman and the spiritual diviners may be. The churinga is a symbol known in primal and oral cultures, but not known to most Westerners. The Artic Eskimo, whose traditional culture is rapidly dissipating, believed in a mythical goddess, half human and half fish, called Sedna or Takanaluk, who lived in a cave under the sea, where she kept the animals of the sea and gave them to the Eskimo who followed the proper rituals. The Plains Indians used the tipi, referred to as teepees by outsiders, which was conical in shape, representing cosmological ideas; its structure represented the native's world or universe. Fire within the tipi represented the Great Mysterious and the smoke going through the hole in the top of the tipi represented liberation. The Navajo tribe, which borrowed and used the tipi, have similar traditions, although their structures are more likely to be round-shaped hogans.

Symbols may be dominant or instrumental, depending on their use in rituals or ceremonies. For example, traditionally, the wearing of the Japanese kimono is an expression of transcendent cultural values and the way they are worn is instrumental. Young Japanese girls are taught to move so that the lines of the kimono are kept straight; only the proper amount of flesh is shown to the public. Further, young Japanese ladies must not step up to another level within a home withour taking their shoes off. They should cover their mouth when they laugh and control their emotions.

Paralanguage

Language use expresses more than the spoken message; there is an intimate connection between body expression and language development. For example, the human voice has acoustic properties, such as speed of talking, pitch or intensity, which condition the message stream and affect how a message is interpreted. An excited voice conveys different information to the listener than does a languorous voice. People determine, often stereotypically, the character or personalities of others based on their vocal patterns. Voices are thought to be sexy, masculine, feminine, weak or strong, based almost exclusively on how they sound to the listener. The trained voice of the opera singer is very different from the voice of the throat singer of a remote tribe, their training being based on very different cultural assumptions.

Researchers indicate that a voice in Western societies conveys masculinity when it resonates strongly; a mellow, more warm voice conveys femininity. Some research suggests that humans have vocal signatures. Indeed, people recognize one another by the vocal patterns being displayed. They know who is on the other end of the telephone without seeing them.

Cultural regions vary paralinguistically. It is shown, for example, that Mediterranean people and people from Latin American countries are more likely to be demonstrative and to use more emotion laden speech than are peopie from English cultures. These are tendencies. Problems arise, of course, when people create stereotypes of others from cultures different from their own. In another vein, the concept of floor management is associated with paralinguistic behavior. People hold and maintain the floor when they interact with others. For example, it has been shown that members of Japanese culture tend to talk simultaneously but that their nonverbal behavior is rhythmic and coordinated . They use back-channeling effectively, letting the other party know that they are listening. Backchanneling can take the form of uh huh or of silent attention.

Because of cultural differences, Japanese and Americans, each unfamiliar with the others' display rules may feel a sense of arhythmicity. Studies show that American males, for example, use more floor space than do females and they tend to be more aggressive in their behaviors, in contrast to the Japanese. Thus, the Japanese and the Americans may use different rules and assumptions about turn-taking, turn yielding and turn requesting, each critical pieces of floor management (Hayashi, 1996). Even using the eyes to signal the end of a turn may vary between cultures.

In Arab countries, loudness may be suggestive of strength and sincerity and softness may suggest weakness and deviousness (Hall, 1966). Members of black communities use pauses differently than do members of white cultures. A faster speed of talking is associated with Latin cultures compared to people in the United States.

The concept of voice-set is important (Pittam, 1994). Two people, perhaps an older person and a younger person, may utter the same phrase, with the same emphasis, but differences will be shown by their set of voice, a fundamental part of their physiological and social development. Age, gender and ethnicity and even the influence of technologies are shown paralinguistically in human behaviors. The role of silence, not well investigated cross-culturally, is keen; by saying and doing nothing, humans influence one another, as in the silent stare of the mother who is disciplining her child. Silence plays an important role in nonverbal communication.

Rituals and Ceremonies

Nonverbal communication involves both individual and collective behaviors. Performative acts, resulting in theatre, ceremony, ritual and spectacle are forms of nonverbal communication that remind people of their culture, their past, present or future, and provide means of identity. Ritual performances in Bali or New Guinea, such as Trance and Dance, may seem bizarre to Americans, but they reveal the power of meaningful ritual to the people involved. The kabuki, in Japan, a shrine-based folk dance and drama, and the Native-American rain dance are familiar to people through movies and television, but most Americans never see in person the more mysterious rituals of people who live in oral cultures.

Rituals are communal activities bonding people together. Just as individual nonverbal communication is often intentional, collective nonverbal communication is intentional although participants may not fully understand the symbolic meanings behind the activity. Most people are familiar with the ritualistic and ceremonial activities found in marriage, courtship and sports activities, but they may fail to see or understand the deeper meaning of these performances, even though they take part in them.

Except in very primal and past-oriented societies, rituals and ceremonies change, especially when Western technology permeates cultures. In societies marked by change, new rituals and ceremonies are invented or old ones are modified. In contrast, oral societies are slow to change; for example, the Yanesha tribes in Amazonia write history into the landscape, using topographs to convey ritual meaning to members of the tribe. The Yanesha are preliterate but their use of topographic writing successfully transmits cultural history and symbols to new members of the culture. Contrast that ritualism with the modern phenomenon called the Rave, where some young Americans ritualistically take part in large musical gatherings, sometimes involving drug use.

Framing Initiation Rituals

In Australia, among the Aranda, male rite initiation includes being tossed in the air and hit with sticks. the young person may be circumcised and the head opened, scarred by having a name carved on the forehead. They may even be smoked and dried out over fires, as part of the initiation rite into manhood. These rituals are used to bind the past and the present together in specific nonverbal ritualistic and collective acts.

In the United States and other countries, hazing can take the form of painful encounter. Outlawed by the military and by many universities and colleges, hazing pain might be psychological or physical. As part of the teenage culture, it may be a way to embarrass a new member of a club, such as making him walk with a can on his head, or, it may be an act of force, requiring the recruit to get drunk by drinking exorbitantly.

Wedding customs contain aspects of ritual and ceremony together, varying widely throughout the world. For example, in times of slavery in the United States, African men and women were not allowed to marry, but a couple could publicly declare their mutual love by jumping over a broomstick to the accompaniment of drums.

Ritualistic, ceremonial collective nonverbal communication exists in all cultures defined by underlying cultural codes, histories and beliefs. They occur in war and in religion; they are part of the daily lives of the members of each culture, binding them to the culture. Such activities may be passed on from generation to generation by story-tellers, shamans, priests and others. In technologically advanced cultures, they are passed along by the media, including libraries. Each generation passes along to the next that which has been received. It traditional societies, the older person passes on knowledge to the young; in modern societies, the young may teach the older person, as is often the situation with the use of computers.

General Environment

While it is true that many preliterate natives or citizens live in cultural environments that have few, if any, modern technologies, most people live in environments that have been influenced by the use of modern technology. The lives of preliterate tribes in the Amazon jungle are very different from the lives of people who live in Hong Kong, Tokyo, Berlin or New York City. All aspects of their existence are different, from food gathering to burial ceremonies.

The general environment deeply influences human behaviors, referring to both the natural world and the social world, interacting together. The reliance upon plants, roots, snakes, bugs and various worms and grubs for food is not uncommon in rural societies where modern, packaged foods do not exist. An example from the Northern latitudes where Eskimos ate whale and seal blubber, used the fur from polar bears and produced burnable supplies of oil from their fat is another contrasting example of the influence of the general environment upon human behavior. In modern Western societies, the influence of the general environment is just as keen, although it may not be so easily discerned. One of the influences is noted in how humans perceive time.

Chronemics

Time, like space, is a hidden dimension affecting nonverbal communication. Western cultures are said to be clock-bound, having a standard meaning for time, a mechanical ideal. Members are clock-bound. For example, people in management positions in the United States often take courses in time management. Vacations, on the other hand, are designed to help people forget the clock. Views of time are shaped by perceptions that are rooted in cultural and social codes. Cultures that focus on the present use objective, linear time. Time in the United States, is a powerful influence on daily behavior.

Scholars suggest that there are many forms of time. For example, there are biological, perceptual, conceptual, psychological and social concepts of time(Bruneau, 1977). Time may be monochronic or polychronic indicating that some societies have a uniform and singular meaning of time while others have multiple meanings. Following this reasoning, people in the United States have a monochronic view of time. Western time begins in Greenwich, England.

By contrast, the Navajo tribe marked time by following the seasons. Watches were not useful in traditional Navajo culture, although that is changing. It is not uncommon for Native Americans, especially those who belong to the Longhouse tradition, to ignore the time of the Christianized White man, who is bound to the clock. Native American children who attend schools in the White world may arrive late following their own time schedule. This behavior, of course, is not designed to disturb teachers or principals. Rather, it reflects how time is conceived in the Longhouse tradition, as on the Iriquois reservation in up-state New York. The author taught Indian children who either came from the Christian or the Longhouse side of the reservation, their values differing accordingly.

On a personal level, people know one another by their use of time. Some arrive at functions typically late or early. Some, as mentioned, seem to function best at night while others go to bed and rise early, like owls or sparrows. Humans have built-in and learned needs that affect how they behave in time. Married partners may be affected badly when one needs only two hours of sleep and the other needs ten! Personal time zones, or individualized ways of viewing time, have been outlined by researchers.

Lower order animal behavior has been studied showing how different species react to time changes. Both diurnal and seasonal changes are expressed in their behaviors, from feeding patterns to denning. Clearly, time and its correlates affect nonverbal communication. Even the aging process is cast in chronology. Time speaks! What it is saying must be interpreted.

Proxemics

With few exceptions, animals defend their territory. Although animals may allow other kinds of species into their territory, they are not likely to permit animals of its own species into that protected territory, especially during rutting or mating season, as in the case of deer. This territorial imperative operates differently in different species. For example, bears and moose range widely, but a chipmunk might stay in a relatively small area for a lifetime.

It is not clear that humans use territories in the same way, although human use of space appears, in some ways, to be an extension of the principle. Humans create national boundaries and they keep enemies out of their territory. Humans put fences between themselves and their neighbors. In short, humans have a sense of home, of place, of situation to which they attach meanings and emotions. Those places may be marked by language usage, by urban buildings or rural fields, by status in community, or by some other means. Humans create and respond to places, such as sacred places, the south versus the north, features in the environment and so on.

Culture influences how humans use space. What is crowding to an American does not appear to be so to a Chinese person, migrating to America, who may choose, perhaps from necessity, to live in very crowded conditions, several persons to a room. Apparently they endure the crowded conditions out of economic need but their cultural norms influence them as well.

Cultures have been described as generally non-contact or contact; that is, some cultures emphasize the need for considerable personal space and others need less. Zero proxemics is a term used to express very close contact between humans. It is said that Latin Americans and Mediterraneans are basically contact cultures while many Western socieites, including Britain, reflect a non-contact orientation. Even intimate eye-contact may be shunned in non-contact countries. Accidental touching in elevators is uncomfortable to many people who are 'civilly inattentive' in the situation.

Geo-techno Dimension

Technological diffusion is reshaping many cultures; as traditional and past oriented societies gain access to modern communicative technologies their social practices are altered. Communicative tools mediate human societies, transforming them. One of the key changes wrought by global technologies, such as the internet, satellites, film and television and the emerging widespread use of the cell phone, is in the concept of geo-techno space. No longer bound by national or regional boundaries, humans can be in touch with others instantly.

Cyberplace, cyberspace, cyberreality are neologisms that reflect the changes that are occurring. It is true that many highly controlled societies, such as the Iraqi and the Chinese or other theocratic countries and groups, such as the Taliban in Afghanistan, do not permit their citizens to interact with others on the internet, nor do they want their people to get their information from the Americans or from some other European media. It is also true that some highly remote tribes and societies do not have access to modern communicative technologies. Nevertheless, the great technological diaspora is reshaping many cultures around the globe.

10

Social Influence on Nonverbal Communication

Humans vary considerably in the ways that they conceive of themselves, in the ways they act, and in the ways that they interpret the behavior of others. Yet, they share intersubjectively in behaviors that are common in their society; otherwise it would not be possible to take part in social networks. The everyday reasoning and construal of the meaning of things is sometimes referred to as a logic-in-use.

Humans strive to make sense of their social worlds; they internalize the meanings that are generated from interaction with others; they make sense of the actions of others; they create lines of action to respond to the perceived demands of a situation. They engage in joint interactions with others. Throughout this process, humans symbolize the self, others and events through perceptual processes. People label the objects of their social world, reflecting their perceptions. By naming things, people frame and interpret them. Human behavior becomes patterned and recognized. Indeed, there is a sociology of the emotions, different patterns of emotional display characterizing various groups in American life. People try to manage their feelings, which, over a period of time reflect patterned ways of dealing with them.

Human relationships are created. For example, partners in a dyadic relationship define their relationship as a kind of symbolic baby. The relationship is something they created together, existing separately from each of the parties. People identify relationships based on their meanings. A special boyfriend treats his special girlfriend differently from the ways that he treats his friends. They respond mutually in terms that they have created, drawing upon their tacit knowledge of expected romantic behavior. It may not be obvious, but each party in a relationship has an implicit set of rules, a definitional frame for that relationship. People sort out what kind of relationship they have with others, which influences how they will behave.

Erving Goffman, a dramaturgist who influenced the growth and development of symbolic interactionist theory, studied the ritualistic nature of human interactions focusing on daily life. He unmasked everyday behavior. He stressed that people have reasons to behave; they performed 'face-work' in their relations with others, exhibiting deference and demeanor. He believed that people try to avoid embarrassment, to meet the perceived expectations of others and the perceived demands of the situation.

Humans may isolate themselves from interaction, developing behavioral and mental symptoms that separate them from others. People may simply withdraw from others, taking the risks involved. Not all people have an 'interaction consciousness' that tells them when an interaction is going well. They can lose "other-consciousness" by being distracted, the result being an unfocused interaction. Goffman developed the dramaturgical metaphor in his analysis of human behavior.

Human behavior is both creative and adaptive but it is their definition of the situation that influences how people will behave. Sociologists who study everyday 'natural' behaviors from an SI perspective attempt to make relevant that which is often obscure. They analyze everyday life, unmasking it, following a logic of implicature, uncovering the deeper meanings to be found in ordinary human events. That which seems to be routine or unimportant to many people may be a rich source of information for the insightful sociologist or analyst.

Symbols

Symbols are created by humans; yet, they may take on a life of their own, used again and again over long periods of time by different members of a society. They are intersubjective, interpretive tools although they may not convey exactly the same meaning to each individual. People are practical semioticians; they symbolically construct the self; they symbolically construct community. It is because humans are fairly predictable about their use of symbols that society has an integrity. For example, the national elections for the president of the United States are predictable because demographers know about the symbolic patterns of the voters, the patterned semantics of being Republican or Democrat.

Humans act in a social world that has been constructed symbolically. Without shared symbolic representations, humans could not interact successfully. That is, all humans create individual meanings for the objects in their world, such as cars, the stock market, schools, families and so on but it is in the intersubjective aspects, the shared aspects of this symbolization, that human interaction is possible. Symbols, by themselves, do not have meaning; the meaning is attached to the symbol by the individual.

New symbols are created to represent new says of thinking about everyday matters. Language, of course, is inherently symbolic. Long ago, Burke described language as symbolic action. Humans symbolize all activities in their lives. They create and share meanings. they engage in an interpretive, sensemaking process. Recently, the Zia Indians in the Southwestern United States, have taken steps to have their sun symbol removed from use by non-native commercial advertisers. The sun symbol is sacred to the Zia but it has been used as a commercial logo by various companies. In short, the Zia native Americans believe that their sun symbol is desecrated when it is used commercially.

Situated Self, Standpoint Theory, Contexts and Codes

Most people in the United States are not born into affluent situations where access to money may be taken for granted. Most people, born into a work-a-day world, need a job to make ends meet. People are situated economically in society. In like manner, they are situated politically, religiously, by gender and ethnicity and by age. Money and influence go hand in hand. Ethnicity, gender and age are embedded in networks of power, or the lack of it.

Power is unequally distributed in the United States, as it is in all countries. The powerful members in society tend to yield their influence on governing boards of major corporations, including the media. They are situated in very different locations in society than is the everyday person. It is this situationism that influences how people think and act. The very wealthy members of society can make choices that are not available to the poor members as in the choices of automobiles, the clubs one joins, the travel that one enjoys and so on. In short, people enact behaviors in keeping with their standpoint in society.

A good illustration is to be found in the history of women and minorities in the United States. They have had less access to power than men have had. In recent years, many women have tried to make up the power difference by collectively creating political and economic organizations that will enable them to present a united front. Women present themselves in accordance with their interpretations of the social situation. Similarly, members of ethnic groups enact communicative behaviors that arise from their situation in society. Their unique social history means that they construe life differently from mainstream Whites. The contexts and social codes influencing the ways they think are different from those of mainline white groups.

For example, Cuban Americans in Little Havana in Miami, have a highly politicized Cuban background. They consider themselves to be political exiles from a hostile Cuba. Many of them were forced out of Cuba or voluntarily fled the country. Their political and economic views and how they make sense of their social worlds, arise from a history that is very different from that of most Americans who were born and raised under calm conditions. Their identity is highly politicized. Their self-identities have been constructed based on their experiences. Their social behaviors arise from their standpoint in society.

The gist of the concept of place is that people create meanings for the places where they have grown up and they are deeply influenced by their sense of place. Humans are affected by night and day, by temperatures of regions, by urban-rural backgrounds and other factors, all of which are associated with the concept of place. Place, of course, varies greatly for different people, some of whom are mobile, while others are fixed in a geographical area.

Some people are cosmopolitan in outlook; others tend to be insular. Thus, for example, one's sense of place may be associated with a small town in Alabama, not far from a large urban setting, which in turn is associated with a southern region where identifiable ways of behaving occur. Context is imbedded in context, each with identifiable social markings.

Agentive and Enactment Processes

Humans act agentively and dramaturgically. That is, they act on their own behalf as though they were performers on a stage. Just as vocalized language rests on a symbolic labeling process, nonverbal communication rests on a symbolizing process. People think about what they will say to an audience in a speech class; they also think about how they will dress or appear in front of that audience. Thus, verbal and nonverbal activities rest on a common interpretive process.

The Chicago School of SI emphasizes agentive role-taking behavior. For example, a student takes notes in class, studies and takes tests; as part of social life, the student may join a fraternity or sorority or sing or dance in a performance. The teacher, on the other hand, probably will do none of the above although, as a student she probably did the same things. Perceiving her role to be professional and authoritative, the teacher provides expert knowledge to the student, separating her out from the students. Faculty members may or may not mix with students, depending on how they construct their relationships with students. In short, students and faculty engage in very different nonverbal role-taking behaviors reflecting their self perceptions and their perceptions of the role they will play in the educational system. Role-taking is a key aspect of SI . The ability to take the role of the other person in interaction is what builds social patterns, groups and institutions.

Framing Society

Any society is built up by the joint interactions of people. Society is really the result of ongoing human interaction. It is constructed by humans; it is maintained by humans; it is changed by humans. Humans engage in joint interactions for a variety of reasons. Perhaps they compromise in one situation; perhaps they pursue goals in another; perhaps they stand aside as others interact, and merely watch. But, social patterns, small and large, stable and dynamic, form society. It is through persisting daily interaction that society is built up.

Roles are not fixed and invariant. They are general and dynamic. Students or faculty members can choose how they will perform the roles, giving it the shape that they prefer. Some faculty members lecture; others engage interactively with students in the classroom. The main point is the faculty member acts as her own agent in the role performance. Roles may be continuous and ongoing or they may be short-lived and terminal.

All people engage in multiple role activities, as students, as parents, as workers, as friends and so on. Humans carry with them the experiences of the past which influence how they interpret and discharge their roles. The demands of the situation are interpreted differently by each individual. For example, one may perceive the role of parenting as a protective one, setting about to protect the child from harm; another may perceive the role as a nurturing one, tending to assist the child in the tasks of childhood. The point, once again, is that the perception of the role to be performed governs how that role will be performed; the baggage, positive or negative, brought from the experiences of the past influence how roles are discharged.

People take into account the many social influences that affect their behaviors in role playing. For example, most students are aware that they should not appear in class naked. Most parents know that they should not beat their children. In short, the underlying social codes, usually not written down, inform people about appropriate role playing behavior. People catch on to the rules. Appearing in class naked will get attention; it may also lead to a sense of embarrassment. The perception of appropriateness is part of the sensemaking process. People model and imitate the performances of others in role-taking behavior.

Dramaturgy

The ways that humans enact or act out their lives both verbally and nonverbally has been called dramaturgical, a metaphor used by Erving Goffman. He observed that people act as though they were on a stage, the stage of life, and as though there were an audience observing them. Humans interact with others, acting out behaviors, and they receive appraisals, good or bad, from their observors or fellow participants in the interaction. Humans attempt to influence others by their nonverbal behaviors. For example, the phrase "She was dressed to kill" is a dramaturgical notion understood by most people. The actor may deliberately "dress to kill" to affect or influence others in a particular way, or she may simply have been ignorant of the social expectations of others. As Goffman pointed out, embarrassment usually results from being ignorant about social expectations.

The important point is that humans often plan to present themselves in specific ways to accomplish specific goals or tasks. They can feign friendship; they may smile to hide deceit; they can smile to attract others; they can smile to impress others. They can "dress to kill". The body "shines" or gives off cues to others; people can choose to direct their presentations in specific ways. People engage in impression management, in self presentation. On occasion, humans act in Machiavellian ways, performing acts to gain an advantage, regardless of the effect on the other parties.

Games and Strategies

The patterned nature of social behavior seems to be game-like when observed from a third-party perspective. For example, the romantic relationship discussed above would appear to be guided by hidden rules and expectations, not unlike the rules of games, such as chess. From a transactional perspective, different from, but not incompatible with SI, a psychiatrist analyzed human behaviors in game terms, suggesting that humans play games in marriages, in sexual relationships, in parties, and in other situations. From this perspective, people put on a game-face and enact roles based on that identity. For example, the female may play the role of a mother and the male may play the child, defining the relationship as a mother-child game, even though two adults are playing the game.There are good games and there are bad games.

Games were important to Mead, the founder of what is now Symbolic Interactionism. Mead believed that childhood games were microcosms of later adult life. That is, he believed that the play of the child contained within it an early understanding of life's rules, expectations and so on. In the playing of games, children create social relationships which may or may not be healthy. For example, it has been suggested in the media that bully behavior on the part of male adolescents may be traceable to the ways that children played games in early childhood. This is probably a common view at a time when adolescent male bullying seems to be on the rise.

Games, of course, have boundaries and rules; people develop skills in playing them whether the result is positive or negative. Some people engage skillfully in interaction with others; others act awkwardly, perhaps suffering embarrassment. People engage in joint activities, in interaction rituals, in ceremonies and in episodic events, seemingly playing the social games of life.

Processes of Socialization

It is safe to say that all nonverbal communication or

behavior is learned through the processes of socialization. Children are directly and indirectly socialized. Few topics have occupied the attention of sociologists as much as the study of socialization processes. People get their values, beliefs, attitudes, behaviors and expectations from early socialization experiences. True, people will modify and re-interpret their experiences as they age, but the basic patterns are rooted in socialization. How much human behavior is influenced by pre-birth conditions is not clear.

For example, it may be that the emotions of a preborn child are influenced by the emotional condition of the mother. An anxious mother may unwittingly pass her anxieties to her unborn child, just as an alcoholic mother may inflict biological harm on the child. Research about these influences is recent and results are unclear. What is clear is that the socialization process is active immediately after birth. The American way of birth is distinctive compared to birthing in earlier societies.

Biology certainly plays a key role in human behavior. Sociobiologists vary in their interpretation of how much the biology and chemistry of the body influences the behavior of the child. The nature-nurture controversy continues. It is argued that any trait that enables humans to survive, to find water, air, food and shelter is likely to influence human behavior substantially. Precisely how the nature-nurture interaction works is not known.

Although children are born with predisposing "biological hardware", they are not 'hardwired' as are most lower order animals. In short, they can create their own sense about the body. Most lower order animals, excepting perhaps chimps and dolphins, do not appear to be able to make sense of themselves; although this, too, is debated. In their situation, biology appears to determine their behaviors. In humans, however, biology is not totally determinative of behavior. People learn to behave. Learning is achieved through socialization processes.

Children catch on to the meaning of things, of events in their lives. They model and imitate their parents, siblings, peers and heroes. Joint social interactions form the foundation for the growth of the child.

Clearly, the human body is a physical organism, having an obdurate character. As mentioned, however, people overlay the body with meaning, symbolizing it. Yet the body appears to grow and change along fairly predictable lines, almost without regard to how humans think about their bodies. However, at each physical growth stage there are companionate social stages. For example, the verbal part of the child's communicative reportoire emerges only after the nonverbal part has emerged. Infants learn to control muscles from the top of the body downward; first learning to use their heads, mouth and eyes, then sitting up and finally standing and walking. Neonates are sensitive to loudness, to the tone of the human voice from early on. In short, early socialization may loaded on the side of the physical body.

People gradually learn about their bodies; they affix meaning to the bodies as they are influenced by various socialization processes. They create body identities. Those who follow Freud's psychoanalytic thinking, might argue that much, pehaps most, nonverbal communication is influenced by unconscious processes; others might argue that underlying, hidden mechanisms, such as the emotions, influence human behavior. But, in the final analysis, it is clear that humans make at least a sketchy sense of their own behaviors and the behaviors of others through the gradual processes of socialization.

Through imitation and modeling, a child may learn to act like his father, a girl like her mother. Cetainly modeling and imitative learning is not linear; rather, it is complex, usually indirect. By seeking out peers later in their lives, children reinforce who it is they think they are. Their self-identity is formative and telogenetic. Throughout their lives, though the various stages of life, individuals attempt to validate who they are, trying to come to terms with their identity.

Growth of Children

Research over the past 30 years shows that, starting as a newly born baby, a human has a strong orientation to others, to their voices, and even to their smells At four months, a child can stick out its tongue in response to the mother and at about 15 months the child can imitate facial expressions of the mother and open its hands in response to adults. Even the facial gestures of the child are influenced by mimicry; happiness, sadness and surprise can be imitated by the young child. It has been noted that even sightless children smile, suggesting perhaps that this activity is innate; however, in sighted life, mimicry plays an influential part.

Modeling involves paying attention to key persons; children see their parental behaviors as examples to be followed. Later, of course, the child will enact her or his own stylized way of communicating nonverbally; yet, the early influences will still be there. Walking, eating, speaking and other important life enhancing activities are given an early push thorugh the modeling process, essentially an interactive process.

Although children act creatively, they are influenced to act in patterned ways, too. Young teenagers, for example, learn how to preen and dress for special occasions, following the lead of their peers. The stuff that becomes internalized is heavily influenced by modeling. Schools, television, play and other processual, ongoing activities serve to influence the child. The child learns to express nonverbal behaviors by taking account of the social exhibits of others. Gradually, the child creates personal schematic lines of action that work successfully in interactive situations.

Play

Children learn to play early in life. It has been said that play is work to the child. Whether it is playing with their food, pretending that a doll is real, or engaging in sport, as mentioned, a child's play is a microcosm of what is to come. In play, children learn to sort themselves out in a form of gender segregation. A budding style of play emerges for each gender. The young girls learns not to be too aggressive; young boys learn to be somewhat aggressive or agonistic. Children learn to take the role of the other in play, seeing that role in the actions of others. They make friends that deeply influence their behaviors.

Joint Interaction

As in primate and other animal behaviors, the newborn is gentled, touched, and cared about so that it can form a trusting bond with its mother. The baby does its part by responding with coos and cries, interacting jointly and intersubjectively with its mother. Although other creatures, such as goslings, form a bond with the object nearest to it at birth, a human child forms an attachment that is more mentative and less hard-wired. Fondling and gentling by the animal mother is demonstrated in nearly all mammalian, four legged and higher order animals. It also characterizes human, mother-child relationships. Gentling and bonding by touching and cooing form attachments at a critical and fragile stage of development for the child.

The early attachment styles of newborns are affected directly by the presence or absence of this mutual bonding process, as mentioned, young children who lack a gentle and caring mother, who may suffer from physical and emotional abuse, may develop dysfunctional attachment styles. It is in this early process of mutual bonding between mother and child that the child begins to sense the importance of its body and of itself. The mother, father and key others begin the socialization process that will lead to identity for the child. In short, the self is not a given; rather, it is forged by learning activities, constructed in interaction with others. Mutuality and intersubjectivity are part of the sharing process. The child learns about meanings, about itself and its importance, about appropriate behaviors and so on. Later, the child is able to label, or symbolize, the world because of its early experiences.

Self and Body Image

Humans are members of the animal kingdom; but, unlike other primates and lower order animals, humans are consciously aware of themselves, taking themselves as objects of their own thought. As a human, a person can say, "I am Johnnie" or "I am Suzie" and have specific ideas in mind about what the name means. Humans construct their identities, achieving a sense of self, which, although it is flexible, contains fairly enduring characteristics. The body, of course, is a critically important part of human identity.

Framing the Self and Identity

People treat themselves as objects and talk about themselves with some certainty. Although the concepts of self and identity have many different interpretations, varying considerably between and among scholars, a symbolic interactionist view is taken. Identity and self, essentially the same concepts, arise in social interaction; they are involved in all human interactions and performances. "As we communicate toward self we are able to see ourselves in the situation, to recognize who we are in relation to others and vice versa, as well as to evaluate our own action in the situation. We are able to judge ourselves and to establish an identity".

Although very early on both genders attach themselves to parents, gender segregation gradually occurs and children gradually become relatively independent. It is said that the colors pink and blue, used at birth to distinguish males and females, sets the tone for later gender development. Through the various stages of life, nonverbal behaviors become genderized.

Although the concept of identity seems to connote an integrity that is played out over a lifetime, some research suggests that the formation of identity may be negatively influenced by a society that is heavily mediated, especially by television. Born with a body, the individual must learn how to make sense of the body and the self; it is more difficult in modern times, some scholars assert.

Thus, through interactions with others, the child learns the meaning of her or his own body. Through praise and criticism, parents reinforce how their children see their own bodies. Saying to the child, "Oh, you are beautiful" is very different from saying "Why don't you dress up more?" implying that the child is less than attractive. Thus children learn about their bodies gradually. If a child learns that his genitalia are dirty, he may become overconcerned about them. Body images, body concepts, body schemes, body attitudes, and body experiences are phrases used to suggest the symbolic nature of the body. The young lady, seeing herself as too fat, believes that others see her as too fat, and acts accordingly. She engages in a type of self-fulfilling prophecy.

Humans go through relatively patterned growth periods, labeled by a number of scholars in varying ways. Clearly, human nonverbal communication changes as humans mature, although behaviors from earlier stages persist. Humans can and do change the way they think about the events in their life. Thus, the gerontological age, for example, is viewed as problematic by some people while it is viewed as an opportunity for further growth by others. People can continue to learn new ways of communicating nonverbally.

The stages of life seem to be fairly predictable in American life and a variety of stage-type theories exist. Although stages are not truly fixed, they are somewhat predictably patterned so that children move from early childhood into pubescence and then into adolescence in varying but fairly routine ways, predicated on physiological development, body changes and so forth. The social and physical growth of the child are intertwined . For example, the child is not able to lift a fork to its lips until its motor skills are developed. A child begins to understand what eating means when its linguistic and cognitive skills are developed. From eating with its hands, the child gradually emerges into full-blown maturity, able to perform complex nonverbal tasks, such as hosting a dinner party or eating in a fashionable restaurant without embarrassing herself. The child learns how to act through a complex interactive set of activities with her parents.

Stage theories are complex, some very popular and well researched; others very hypothetical. In every situation, at whatever stage, humans try to interpret and make sense of their status; in many cases, rites-de-passage mark a stage, such as coming out parties, or retirement parties. Parents watch their children grow from the neonatal stage, through adolescence to older age. Although parents have gone through various life stages, they may be unnerved by the behaviors of young teens, whose lifestyles may be radically different from their parents. Later, the parents will be grandparents, which calls for a very different set of expectations and behaviors. All people pass through life's stages; at each stage, the individual must make sense of the social world, coming to terms with her or his identity. Their social behaviors, their interactions with others are displayed accordingly.

Nonverbal Competence and Self Presentation

Recent research emphasizes the agentive role of humans, starting with children, who learn to act on their own behalf. Children are not "developed" so much as they create ways of seeing the world and ways of acting. They enact themselves, becoming quickly attuned to their circumstances. Children become competent at nonverbal tasks as practical achievements, from playing ball, to later courtship activities. Parents, not usually trained experts in the raising of children, use a folk-type model to guide them. Children learn from a type of teleogenetic process deriving meaning from small action events. For example, when a child is praised for the way she or he handles a fork or spoon, the child is likely to continue to use it in skilled ways. Eating such a thing as a boiled egg, pealing it and then consuming it can be a complex event for a young child. The child must work the mind, eye, hand and mouth together to perform what later will be a simple, routine task.

Children learn to present themselves based on what they have learned. They learn to dress, finding out what dress codes are all about. They learn when to smile and when to frown. They create a reportoire of skilled competencies in a presentational style. Their gestures are used to create impressions and to influence people and their general body language becomes part of their communicative package. Studies of feral children reveal how important human socialization is to the child. "Wild" children are stunted in physical, emotional, intellectual and social growth; they cannot symbolize human events appropriately.

Action Theory and Networking

When humans engage in action, they usually know something about why they are doing it and what the likely outcomes will be. The tasks they perform may be very simple or very complex. A simple task might include putting on the right shoes; a complex task might include walking in those shoes to make a sale as a professional staff member of a major commercial company. In each case, people attach meaning to what they are doing, symbolically. Even friendships are formed symbolically; the dyadic relationship is built upon shared activities, perceived symbolically as part of the relationship.

The ability to manage relationships competently, to be accepted and to do appropriate things to maintain the relationship is the foundation of effective networking. One learns to play roles and enact lines of action, which are recognized by others and incorporated in the relationship. One learns how to dress, how to behave appropriately and how to make a good impression on others. One learns to play roles, some of them continuous. For example, being a parent is a continuous activity; frying an egg is discontinous. Playing the part of a mommy or daddy as a child becomes a precursor to the later performance of parenting. These early enactments teach the child how to behave socially, making networking possible.

Interaction and networking form the crucible of identity formation. Interaction and networking with others is foundational to society as well, without which society could not exist. Patterns of association vary by gender, by age and by ethnicity. Modern communicative technologies offer new ways for people to network with one another, whether in work or play.

Institutional Influence

It is in peer groups that boys and girls learn to identify

themselves. Each person is deeply influenced by the members of groups. Young people know what is "in" and what is "out" and in the teenage years, they are careful to follow the acceptable patterns, for fear that they may become stigmatized or even ostracised from the group. Members of the group may find reason to label and ostracize a person, keeping him or her out of the group because they do not appear to fit the social paradigm.

Members of peer groups create labels for various kinds of behaviors, which become identifying keys associated with each member. For example, one member may be the brain or egghead; another may be "Miss Popularity". The references are to the style of behaviors that each person exhibits. The power of peer groups to influence how members feel and think is enormous, as it is in the workplace.

Group Influences

Small and large groups are network structures, the structures created by humans in interaction. Research suggests that the communicative design of the group influences how people relate to one another. For example, when people sit in a simple circle design, equality is promoted among the members of the group; a wheel design with spokes tends to promote the leader who sits in the central position, through whom most messages must go; the Y pattern usually includes a leader at the bottom end of the Y; the chain style of group activity limits conversations except with the person on either side, or on the left or right side, depending on which end the member is sitting; the all-channel group pattern permits all people to talk to all others equally. Morale is promoted more in the all channel group than it is in the wheel or Y pattern.

Performing effectively in the workplace requires skilled nonverbal behavior. Indeed, it is in the workplace where humans present themselves with some expertise. An engineer, for example, follows lines of conduct associated with his or her discipline, as does the medical doctor. In short, the socialization process does not end at early adulthood; it continues throughout life. The manager of people in the workplace must possess a leadership reportoire. Leaders, of course, are not born; they construct themselves. Not only must the manager have the ability to lead, or manage, but she or he must appear to lead. The boss's office is usually bigger than those of her support staff. The office usually reflects power and influence, in both direct and subtle ways.

For example, the leader's desk may be considerably larger than the desks of the support staff and the office may be furnished with other symbols of the leader's social status. These obvious differences are important to the maintenence of power; yet, the manager must earn the image of being a leader by doing little things to shape an image, such as displaying personal plaques and awards on the wall behind her and taking part in only limited ways in the understaff's activities, distancing herself from them. Bosses and understaff members must learn appropriate roles and behaviors to communicate successfully. Indeed, they must plan to be effective. Managers and other professional people must nurture their image to conform to professional expectations.

Group Activities

In face-to-face dyadic situations, people usually present themselves in the full view of the other participant. In this situation, verbal and nonverbal interactions are easily observed and when the dyadic relationships is balanced, fair play takes place. In imbalanced dyads, however, one person may try to take advantage of another. For example, the young and the old are particularly persuasible; they are easy to influence, sometimes negatively. The more powerful person in the dyad combines nonverbal acts with verbal acts, she or he can persuade the weaker party to do things. The dynamics of groups are influenced by group size.

Law of Numbers

Is there a law of numbers at work in groups? Dyads, for example, consist of two persons where interactions are very different from the three person group, which is very different from much larger groupings. In a dyad one party may play a game of one-ups-manship, trying to better the other person in the dyad. In a three party group, two people can gang up against one in a coalition, which cannot be done in a dyad. In larger groups, people can create subgroups, which influence how behaviors are managed. Subgroupings can develop in 12 member groups but they cannot form in dyads. In a monad where there is but one person, the individual can hold conversations only with the self. The size of the group influences how people will behave.

Joint interactions are the glue of society. Their continuous flow make up the structures of the wider society, which, when formed, influence the individual. Thus, it is a circular process. The wider society is formed by the micro-enactments of small groups, which, in turn, influence the individual. As mentioned; even romantic relationships, which appear to be free-floating to the individuals involved, are deeply influenced by underlying social codes; lovers in American society follow fairly scripted behaviors as they enact their relationship, their symbolic baby, as it were.

Group dynamics pressure members to conform. As mentioned, nonverbal behaviors may become stigmatized or shunned if they do not conform. Many youth groups, for example, shunned by mainline society, form negative images, continuing as identity groups. Skinheads, religious cults, gangs and other types of groups create identities to make a statement to the wider society. Interestingly, these groups, appearing to be nonconformist, often require strict conformity from their members. Further, their relationship to the wider society is somewhat predictable. Riding a motorcycle with black jacket, long dirty hair and dark glasses is almost a guaranteed way to be arrested in many places in the United States.

Familial Influences

The family is an example of a small group which, as in the spoked wheel example, can be highly structured and authoritarian, or it may be flexible, as in the all-channel example. Varieties of family styles exist and the communication patterns vary by type of family. Size of the family influences relational patterns as well. Modern families may have dinner in front of the television set thereby limiting their conversations. Families are small communities constructed symbolically, Family members create meanings that they share intersubjectively, binding them together, some loosely, others tightly.

Families are co-constructed by the members; it is heavily influenced by the wider community as well. In recent America, the diverse forms of the family seem to be increasing. for example, there are: first-marriage families, single-parent families; stepfamilies; cohabiting couple families; geographically separated families; extended families; and, binuclear families in which two nuclear families share their lives with one another. The situation in which women breed children by artificial insemination or in which two people of the same sex marry and adopt children is emerging.

In short, American families have new forms. The family, of course, is influenced by social, religious, political and economic processes in American society. For example, elderly people, formerly attached to their family through a kinship ethos are now more likely to live by themselves or in homes for the elderly than they are to live in the extended family. The family, of course, is the main influence on the behavior of the child. Face-to-face interactions, deeply formed feelings, rules and expectations, and other influences are designed to help the child become an adult in an appropriate way. Yet, the family is itself undergoing major changes in American society and in other technologically developed countries.

Traditional family dinner patterns are giving way to discursive patterns of behavior. The laissez faire family seems to be an emergent form in contemporary American society. The patterns of interaction found in traditional families are far different from those found in laissez faire families. Many families in the United States are fractured, resulting in new and different pressures on the family members. A recent University of Chicago survey says that only one in four American families is considered to be traditional, down 45 percent from the early 1970's. Single earner families, where parents are married and together, are now the exception.

Given the rapid changes in society and the consequent changes in the family in the United States, the processes of identification for children, who are often "stepchildrenized" ,may be disrupted and dysfunctionality may be unwittingly promoted. Children must define themselves in the light of new situational and structural influences, as families dissolve, divorce, or separate. For example, parents with small children who divorce go through stages of dissolution in which "grave dressing" acts influence children, whose loyalties to one parent or the other are shaken. Regrettably, the grief of parents in divorce affects how their children perceive the family. Infants, of course, form emotional bonds of attachment.

When these are disrupted, children may become anxious, ambivalent or avoidant, carrying these emotional feelings into future situations and relationships.

Creation of Relationships

Humans create relationships. They maintain them symbolically. To maintain relationships, humans go through daily rituals. Partner interaction becomes somewhat routinized on a daily basis. Couples may shop on Mondays, go out to dinner on Fridays, visit friends on Saturdays and so on. They may create special events or special holiday practices, such as family reunions, Christmas festivities, or birthday celebrations on a regular basis, as a couple. Couples create places for privacy, such as the bedroom, and places for public interaction, such as the family room. They also create rules of engagement, scripts for undertaking situations of disagreement, for interacting with each other's friends, and so on.

Romantic relationships embody distinct notions, different from other relationships. The behaviors that earmark romance are lodged in the sense of romance that Americans share. The old fashioned idea of a knight on a white horse who rescues a forlorn damsel no longer applies; however, romance embodies notions about sharing that other dyads do not share. The level of intimacy that characterizes romantic relationships is itself governed by implicit rules of touching, which are governed by the experiences of the couples.

Conservative, religious people may decide that sexual consummation is to be withheld until the couple is joined in marriage; other, less conservative young people, may plunge into the sexual act on the first night. The rules of the dyadic relationship must be defined. However they decide to act, as mentioned, they create a symbolic "baby", the relationship. Underlying, often hidden, codes of conduct influence all relationships. People may agree or disagree about how these codes are to be interpreted, but they must admit their presence and their influence on human behaviors.

Face-to-Face Interaction

It is important to reinforce the ideas behind the concept of face, noting that the concept plays a part in all human behaviors. Because the presentation of self is often conceived of as basically dyadic or small group experience, a way of displaying personal identity to others, it is easy to overlook the fact that it is involved as well in routinized patterns of behavior and in public activities.

Routinized Behaviors

As people age, they return again and again to behaviors that have been used successfully before. Lines of action that have served well in the past continue to be used. One does not have to learn how to shake hands after learning it the first time, although one may have to learn about greeting habits in other cultures when traveling between cultures. When nonverbal activities become routinized, they can be performed with little attention required. People may brush their teeth or brush their hair but be thinking about many other things, perhaps planning the day. As mentioned, humans tend to ignore the fact that routines are achieved. Yet routinization is foundational to the creation of society.

Routine Performances

Clearly, humans conduct their activities using simple gestures and complex lines of action. Because they are so common, people tend to overlook their value to society. People drive on the right side of the road in the United

States; to do otherwise would be to undermine the road rules. Not only do people avoid accidents by using a shared road code, but they obey the established laws, which themselves have been socially constructed. Further, the driving venture is part of an interaction ritual that is known to most people in the United States. Driving a car successfully is but one ritualized activity, an example of the multitudes of rituals that form the basis of society. Everyday rituals and routines are full of meaning.

Contingent Behavior

During the day, especially in novel situations, people both give and respond to others, following a contingent pattern; that is, they do something in response to what others have done, or in response to what they think others will do. People take turns enacting behaviors. A smile may create a smile in the other party. If the boss dresses in a suit and tie, the employee responds in kind. In short, people act contingently, dynamically in response to the behavioral enactments of others. In routinized behavior, however, this creative contingent element may be missing. The behavior is relatively fixed and repetitive with no need to change it. Mindful attention is not needed, as it is in novel situations.

Public Displays

Throughout the stages of life, people engage in public displays and ritualizations, whether they are religious, associated with work and play, or secular. Marriage, graduation ceremonies, worship services, concerts and other collective activities contain formulations of appropriate public behaviors. They contain collective scripts for people to follow. Highly symbolic, they reach into the psyche deeply to influence thought and behavior. Marriages may be performed underwater or from a dive out of an airplane, illustrating how times change; yet, there is a symbolic constancy associated with each ceremony. Indeed, a large part of human lives are played out in public ceremonies, themselves value laden, imbued with beliefs and expected behaviors and outcomes.

Until recently, SI scholars have differed in the past about how they view these processes. Some researchers have focused on the macro aspect of social processes while others focused on the micro aspects. At present, there seems to be an attempt to blend the different approaches. Micro processes refer to daily interactive experiences in dyadic or small group situations. Meso processes refer to interactions in larger settings, such as work and school activities, where many people interact. Macro processes refer to those public, society-wide processes that are ongoing, forming the essential character of a society. For example, power is distributed thoughout American society, but it is distributed unevenly. The master themes listed above are macro themes. Macro themes and processes are dynamic, not fixed, although they are somewhat stable. They pervade society at every level, from monadic, dyadic, to group and institutional levels and to national levels. They creep into daily behaviors. Indeed, every society must contend with these master themes.

Even when people engage in self conversations they wittingly or unwittingly take account of these themes. For example, females think differently about events than do males; members of ethnic groups think about ethnicity differently than do white males. The media, of course, display sex and gender themes continuously, as do the film and print media; even the internet is used to promote sexual themes. Communicative technologies clearly influence members of society, framing the master themes. Humans are caught up in powerful social matrices that influence nonverbal communication.

Ethnic Behaviors

Ethnicity is symbolically constructed; it is a dynamic concept. Ethnicity is lived. Unfortunately, social barriers are created when artificial boundaries are erected between ethnic groups. Economic disadvantage frequently serves to mark boundaries between ethnic groups. The construal of ethnic identity in the modern bicultural or multicultural American world often carries the problems of the past into the present.

Fortunately, a new awareness, an interethnic identity seems to be emerging in modern America, although there are destructive elements remaining. The demography of the United States is changing dramatically. The 2000 census shows that Hispanics and Blacks each now represent about 13 percent of the population of the United States. To the extent that access to political, economic and educational institutions is denied them, problems are created by those who hold power.

Regional Influences

Food use is but one behavior that is influenced by region. Dress, speech, beliefs and other behaviors, are influenced as well. Indeed, buying habits, use of language, education levels, attitudes, beliefs and all nonverbal activities are somewhat influenced by the social dynamics associated with a geographic place. The sense of identity is rooted in the sense of geographical place, in a familiar milieu. People tend to network and interact with other people who share broadly their outlooks and aspirations. There are people, of course, who spend considerable time trying to escape stereotypes associated with regions.

Everyday, individuals are called upon to perform, to act as agents, to play various roles and to engage in joint interactions with others. Slowly and gradually, people learn how to act so as not to embarrass themselves, to behave according to hidden social codes. Underlying social codes influence human behavior; however, the codes are forgiving in that they permit a variety of adaptive modes of behavior. The hidden rules are not usually directly impressed on people. They are often caught rather than taught, as the saying goes. They are not obviously manifested and certainly, in an open society, they are not written in stone.

However, there are settings in American society where codes are made fairly explicit. An inmate in a prison, a total institution, has very little freedom to make choices about the activities in his life. Inmates know at all times what the institution requires them to do. The rules are explicit. When the inmate eats, where he goes, and what he does are all controlled by prison officials. Social codes are impressed upon the inmate. In most circumstances, however, one finds a relatively fluid situation in which the expectations, prescriptions and proscriptions of behavior are open and lax.

A middle range of prescription is found in medical and legal settings where codes of behavior are clearly expressed. Judges, for example, do not wear colorful costumes, nor do doctors wear street clothes. In short, these professional settings have manifest codes understood by people who work in the setting. In other settings, of course, such as in some religious schools, one is in a clothes-controlled environment and everyone, male or female, wears the same colors and schemes. The uniform hides the backgrounds of the individuals so that both rich and poor dress the same. In brief, the examples used reveal the power of the social milieau to influence the display of nonverbal behaviors.

11

Ethnicity and Nonverbal Communication

Ethnic groups around the world have been mistreated by those in power. Human history in many ways is the history of struggle, as ethnic groups around the globe will attest. There is no attempt to moralize about what happened in early America; nor is there an attempt to malign members of any group. Rather, the attempt is to describe the harsh conditions in which members of ethnic groups struggled as they construed the meaning of life, their own identities. In present-day American society, much of the ethnic turmoil is couched in that history.

New generations of the ethnic groups discussed here confront a different social milieau. There is occasional outright hostility but there seems to be progress in human relations. Yet, stereotypes and other demeaning characterizations appear, often in subtle forms, indicating that the color barrier has not been completely crossed or erased. Barriers to interaction are not caused by one party or the other; they are caused by both or all parties. It would seem that the egalitarian ethos can be realized only when members of each group are inter-ethnically adaptable. The colors red, black, brown, yellow and white are mere surface features in the identification process. By appreciating these human colors rather than derogating them, people can do productive ethnic borderwork.

A Historiographic Approach of Ethnic Identity

School children, born and raised in the United States, have been taught that the United States is the land of freedom, that others from countries around the world are welcome to these shores, whether they were immigrants from war-torn countries or others who came here to make a better living, to live the good life. The egalitarian ethos is a powerful theme, appreciated first by the religious Whites who came to these shores to gain religious freedom. Although it serves as a reminder of opportunity in America, many people have not benefited.

All creatures, including humans, were located on a hierarchy. White European males were placed on the highest level in this hierarchy; women were placed below men and people of color; animals occupied the lowest levels. The separation of the races was promoted; distorted versions of Darwinism, scientific racism and eugenics were sometimes linked together in support of racism This theory, along with other beliefs, of course, had dire consequences for people of color in early America.

Monogenetics and Polygenetics

A monogenetic or a polygenetic approach to the classification of human beings was used in early analysis. Under the monogenetic concept, all humans were thought to be the same, following various Biblical injunctions; under the polygenetic concept, races were thought to be distinct, separate from one another. Polygenism was popular in America and it had implications for the status of African slaves. Since, the theory "proved" that whites were different from blacks, qualitatively, it seemed as well that there was a legitimate scientific justification for slavery. Early American thought seemed to be along the following lines.

Evolution leads to diversification and complexity, not to sameness, unless humans live in very strict isolation. Thus the tripartite categorization of races is hardly a scientific classification. When blood types and DNA are brought into the equations, racial categorization is even less scientifically useful. The color of the skin becomes a mere surface feature.

The complexity of intermixed features found among humans throughout the world is now obvious; racial categorization is fraught with difficulty. However, this fact did not historically prevent some scientists from attempting to classify races by intelligence. Indeed, one of the motives for classification was to show the racial superiority of the white person. Phrenology, unacceptable today as a scientific tool, was used to show how races differed from one another according to brain size. Brain size, however, is not a good indicator of intelligence, once again showing how some scientists were misguided.

The concept of ethnicity is probably more modern than is the concept of race. For example, the early British appeared to be more involved with ideas about loyalty, honor, connection, station and conformity that it was with ethnicity. Race refers mostly to physical characteristics while ethnicity refers to socially learned behaviors, passed on from one generation to another, often modified in the process. In early American history, the word ethnic was used to label minorities as "heathens", as perceived by white people. Today, ethnicity refers to a wide range of characteristics that are associated with groups, such as social customs and foodways. To describe oneself in ethnic terms can be a positive way for humans to identify themselves.

Framing Black Nonverbal Styles

Rather than just walking, Blacks seem to move rhythmically. When young Blacks bop down the street, it is a statement of identity, of self-power. Wearing clothes is a way to make a statement about self-identity; it is a way of giving force, or Nommo, to one's life. Shades, or dark glasses, may be worn to provide some magic. Sometimes showboating, or verbal boasting, as Muhammed Ali did, is performed to make a statement. An individual style is highly preferred and respected among blacks, so commonly found in their musical expressions. Black performers want to use distinctive skill and style, not machine-like performances.

Ethnic identity is a social construction, created by humans to give meaning to one's life. Skin color may be a part of the identification process but it is not the key part. It is through the taking of roles that one construes who she or he is and those roles are influenced by early upbringing, by association with others who hold similar beliefs and attitudes. Shared world views, shared social practices and commonality of experience are part of ethnic construction.

Interethnic problems result when people define themselves too rigidly. In other words, ethnicity is Janus-faced; it builds a sense of community, but at the same time, it can separate one from the wider society. Ethnocentrism and xenophobia are indicators that members of a rigidly constructed ethnic group may feel threatened, even paranoic about the wider culture. Whether these groups are White supremacists, Black Muslims, or members of Chinese gangs, their rigid positions thwart their acceptance into mainline culture. Numerous factors, such as power, gender, sexual orientation and social class influence the construal of the lives of members of ethnic group members.

Ethnic Differences

Language is a marker of identity, a fact that made members of these groups stand out from the early white Americans; often, it made it easier to make strangers of them. Older members of these four groups tend to maintain their language faithfully; very young ones may speak English outside the home while speaking the traditional language at home. Many Navajo children have lost the Navajo language; it is not always passed down from elders to children.

Interestingly the Navajo language, oral and pictographic, and not written down until recently, was used in modified form to create a secret code during World War II when code talkers of Navajo background were used as message bearers. The Navajo language, scarcely known to most Americans, was completely unknown to the Japanese, who could find no way to decipher the code. Trained as message bearers, the Navajo code talkers successfully transmitted commands from military headquarters to troops on the front lines. All languages are codes, of course, but the distinctive linguistic characteristics of the Navajo language were extraordinarily useful as a unique code in wartime.

Blacks brought to America for slave purposes as part of the slave trade, came from a rich, diverse panoply of local and regional dialects and languages. Thus, often they were not able to communicate among themselves due to these differences. Shipmasters mixed together blacks who spoke different dialects to help prevent them from banding together in an uprising. Even today, Blacks may speak in very distinctive ways, as the Ebonics movement revealed.

Black slave history meant that the slaves would receive little or no education or training. It also meant that they would develop distinctive features in their spoken English, many of which survive in modified form to this day. The Black church, often outlawed, became the focal point for gatherings of black folk. They learned very expressive ways to sing and dance using their own stylized languages.

The immigrating Chinese, arriving over a period of time from different parts of China, were multi-lingual, a factor contributing to their complex history. The Chinese language is monosyllabic, unlike English which is polysyllabic. To provide variety and complexity to the language, Chinese people use tonal levels to differentiate one word from the next, resulting in a sing-song quality, as many Americans perceive it. Major linguistic groups, such as Cantonese and Mandarin, existed, mostly centered in various geographic regions of China. Even within these major linguistic groups, one region would vary from another in the way that words were spoken. Thus, the Chinese who came to America in the mid-1800's brought different dialects with them, depending on the area of China from which they came.

Today, young Chinese Americans born in the United States learn English, although they may speak it with some phonetic difficulty because the Chinese spoken at home is radically different from spoken English. Hispanics from Cuba spoke a modified version of traditional Spanish imported from Spain; however, it was admixed with the linguistic varieties of Indian and Black dialects. Thus, it was distinctive. English is spoken in Cuba as well, the U.S. having taken Cuba from Spain during the late 1800's and the flow of commercial traffic that existed before Castro encouraged the use of English. Cuba, centered in the Caribbean, became a crossroads, a place of conquest, as the Spanish-American war demonstrated. Young Cuban Americans, born in the United States, frequently speak fluent English, although their parents and grandparents may speak only broken English.

Fortunately perhaps for them, Spanish is more compatible with English tha is either Chinese or Navajo; it is no accident that Spanish is the language of choice for white students in colleges and universities, where a second language is usually required. Although linguistic distinctiveness is often cited as the main factor in ethnic identity, it is not the sole factor. Ethnicity is expressed as a dynamic flow of verbal and nonverbal clusters of behaviors, including individual and public displays. Having a background of similar values, customs, habits, beliefs and so on, members of ethnic groups tend to express themselves in recognizable ways, individually and collectively. American Standard English is taught in schools which brings up an issue of conformity. The issue seems to be whether linguistic diversity is desirable in American society.

When Columbus arrived in the Western world, there were an estimated two million Indians, named so because Columbus thought he had discovered a new route to the Eastern world; the Indians did not call themselves Indians. The Navajo, for example, referred to themselves as Dine. They had come apparently from the Canadian North; they lived in a natural relationships with the earth, the moon, the sun and the stars. Over the years, they had been hunters and gatherers, agriculturalists and pastoralists. The Spanish brought the horse to their civilization.

Their religious way of life was distinctive, rich and full. Man was to live in tune with nature and with his fellow man. Singers and chanters told stories about their past and conducted healing ceremonies. Great ceremonies included masquerades, dance, prayer and song. There was little distinction between the sacred and the profane. Witchcraft was practiced, too. The early Navajo believed that it was possible to influence the course of events by means involving the supernatural. Prayers were silent and mental prayers or monologically expressed with short devotional repetitions.

The Navajo did not distinguish strictly between maleness and femaleness; tied into some of their myths were stories about hermaphrodites which symbolically united males and females. Weavers, often women, wove symbols and stories into the patterns. In short, the Navajo had a meaningful and established cultural identity; they lived in a place between the mountains and hills, an earthly but spiritual home, a sacred place.

It was highly unfortunate that for the white man, the general image of the Navajo was as an uncultured savage, whose cosmologies were mysterious, whose practices were foreign to the mind of the white man, perhaps even threatening. White Americans had very different goals and ways compared to the the Navajo. The white man at least had a pretense of science, but the Indians lacked that sense. Indians tended to see forces in nature that could help or hurt them. They considered it necessary to appease and get along with the spirits that existed. By using prayers and ritual forms, the Indian could get the spirits to work with him, rather than against him. The Christian white man did not share these approaches to nature. The Christian God was his benefactor as he took charge of the lands through which he moved.

In military clashes, the dominant white man prevailed over time. A popular slogan says that it is the powerful, the winners, who write the history of peoples and they write those histories from their own perspectives. It was the White man who imposed his will and hoped to impose his culture upon the Navajo using a variety of methods, perhaps believing that he was doing the "right" thing. Surely, he was doing the expedient thing because, as the White man moved west, he wanted more and more land.

After the United States annexed the Southwest, white contacts with the Navajo increased. Considered intruders by the Navajo, Whites nevertheless destroyed their orchards and their sheep herds, in a raid by Kit Carson, to whom they surrendered in 1863. The Navajo tribal members were rounded up, except for those who fled to the hills, and marched to Bosque Redondo, a very distant desert site the government had selected to force them into farming, into irrigating the land. This farming experiment failed and they were forced onto reservations in a new policy designed to civilize them. The Navajo tribe resisted this effort, although it eventually succeeded. The Whites believed they had to civilize the savages. The Navajo spirit was shattered.

Deep, great changes were wrought in Indian tribal affairs by the arrival of whites and their contact with them, often to their own detriment and denigration. Too often, the Indians had become a problem for the whites and, eventually, even the use of Reservations to solve these problems were failures, by and large. Not only were wars fought to contain the Navajo, but diseases, such as smallpox and influenza for which the Indians had no remedy-- for these were diseases of the White man—destroyed many. It also tended to destroy or render inoperative the Indians control over the supernatural and to trigger changes in their 'ecosystem', as it did among most Indian tribes. The Bureau of Indian Affairs, formed in 1890, was designed to change the Indian culture, to "civilize" them. In so doing, they destroyed the will of the Navajo, leaving them little or no political power.

American society is economically stratified rfesulting in the marginalization of many people, often people of color. Despite the progress that has been made in ethnic relations, a recent poll suggests that blacks feel more discriminated against than any other racial or ethnic group. Eighty three percent of the people questioned said that blacks were more discriminated against than were Hispanics, at 76 percent. Women and American Indians were next with 67 percent of those questioned. Further, while whites were quite satisfied with their earnings and where they live, only 49 percent of Blacks reported satisfaction with their household income.

Ethnicity is a nonverbal entity; that is, it is a lived identity, expressed in everyday life, a master theme. It is a complex notion, contrary to the stereotypes often associated with it. There are many symbolically ethnicized voices in America; they are on the increase. The future mosaic of culture in the United States will be complex, full of many different voices, each seeking access to mainstream America. Not only are there symbolic voices but there are lingual voices. Increasingly, people who speak a non-English language are entering the United States. The United States is now multilingual.

Perhaps every nation on earth is represented in the population of the United States. Just how the egalitarian ethos will play out among these groups is not clear. If citizens are to achieve true egalitarianism, wherein any person has access to achievement and privilege, new ways of viewing ethnicity need to occur. Ethnic markers need to be appreciated, not derogated.

Racism

Racism is a cognitive trap that needs to be dismantled if the egalitarian ethic is to work. One need not moralize to realize that Americans have created ethnic traps. But, of course, being different does not have to result in stereotypes or social traps. It is not easy, of course, to recognize cognitive biases or to accept the fact of their existence. It is far easier to continue perceiving the social world in familiar ways. Blacks and whites may be separated physically but they are also separated symbolically. The cognitive trap is symbolic, found in the ways that people think about themselves and others. Closing the cognitive trap may mean resocializing the mind, reconfiguring perceptions, not being blind to self and others.

Interethnic Adaptability

Human behavior is complex and varied; although it appears to be somewhat stable, human behavior may be modified slowly, sometimes with speed. Indeed, to be educated is to be open to change. Change occurs best when a person becomes aware of himself, when optional ways of viewing the world are noted and acted upon. Formal education can help people understand the complex dynamics of ethnic relationships. Not realizing that words are mere representations, humans may think in relatively fixed terms. But inter-ethnic adaptability requires polysemous skill; cross-ethnic friendships are promoted when people can get past judgements that block understanding. Stereotypes are signs that people have closed their minds to important information.

Unmasking Unconscious Perceptions of People of Color

It is not uncommon for one person to socially categorize another person, using fixed perceptual lenses. This would be a harmless process if it did not result in negative consequences for the other party. By labeling people who are different from themselves, calling them stupid or dumb, or niggers or some other stigmatic term, it is unlikely that the name-callers will identify with those people in the future. People become socially ostracized when fixed labels are applied to them. Others use the stigmatic label in copycat ways. Although many of the ways that people relate to one another nonverbally arise from an awareness of self in relation to others, many behaviors are habituated and unconsciously enacted; people often do things while not realizing that they are doing them. Hidden scripts get played out.

Unfortunately, bad habits may be unconsciously performed. For example, white and black people may have fears about one another without realizing it. Fear about an object, a person or an event, can lead to self-protective behaviors. The presence of fear in interethnic relationships can present serious problems. It is not uncommon for white people to fear black people or vice versa. These attitudes are formed from a long history of oppressive conditions, carried forward to modern generations. Race relations in today's America are defined by daily experiences, in schools and sports, in worship and in the workplace.

The study of listening is stressed in recent research. It is commonly thought that listening is the absence of speech or talk, but listening is a nonverbal activity that is profoundly proactive. That is, listening is a deliberate process in which humans focus upon the symbolic behaviors of themselves and others. Real listening is not merely an aural activity, it is a symbolic activity, it is a meaning- making activity. For example, observing and listening are powerful tools in the repertoire of professionals in clinical therapy; this is because so much of the meaning of what people say and do is found "between the lines", not always in what people say but in what they do.

The art of listening is a skilled behavior that is learned. It is very different from hearing, which is a physical activity, tied into sound and vocality. Effective listening includes interpretive theories that get at what a person is really saying or doing. An empathic listener focuses on the pains that a person feels as she describes a loss of a friend, responding with empathy. The non-sympathetic listener hears the words, but misses the hidden meanings. It is no accident that marriage counselors focus on the failure of men to really listen to their wives, or vice versa, to note what is really going on between them that is causing problems.

Good listeners can be good problem solvers because they focus on what is really happening. They can reconcile differences between themselves and others because they know where the important aspects of the relationship lie. They build bridges, not walls. Good listening skills do not mean that there is a one way street in nonverbal communication. It is an interactive process. Good listening practices allow people to agree or disagree but to still take part in the interaction in meaningful, important ways. Effective disagreement can be healthy and it can help promote quality relationships. Quality listening is a powerful tool for ethnic borderwork.

12

Public Relations

Public relations (PR) is the aspect of mass-marketing that deals with the control or manipulation of public opinion, through processes that control the presentation of the image and message presented by a client. Public relations agents or "officials" make use of media to convey messages to the public on behalf of a private client, with the intention of influencing public opinion and action. Organizations that seek to profit from the mass market, may view the public relations as a valuable aspect of an overall business and marketing strategy.

PR agents deliver info to the media directing their messages toward wider audiences, or to limited demographic segments within the public, called "target audiences" -usually defined based on market research. Research may deal with product appeal, target demographic modeling, as well as strategies for coordinated message presentation. Similar opinions tend to be shared by a group of people rather than an entire society, however, by targeting different audiences with different messages to achieve an overall goal, PR practitioners can effect widespread opinion and behavior change. PR is essentially the privatized decendant of "propaganda," which now normally refers to mass-scale message control by state and national governments.

History of Public Relations

The precursors to public relations can be found in the publicists who specialized in promoting circuses, theatrical performances, and other public spectacles. Many PR practitioners have also been recruited from the ranks of journalism and have used their understanding of the news media to ensure that their clients receive favorable media coverage.

The First World War also helped stimulate the development of public relations as a profession. Many of the first PR professionals, including Ivy Lee, Edward Bernays, and Carl Byoir, got their start with the Committee for Public Information (also known as the Creel Committee), which organized publicity on behalf of U.S. objectives during World War I. Some historians regard Ivy Lee as the first real practitioner of public relations, but Edward Bernays is generally regarded today as the profession's founder.

Ivy Lee, who has been credited with developing the modern news release, espoused a philosophy consistent with what has sometimes been called the "two-way street" approach to public relations, in which PR consists of helping clients listen as well as communicate messages to their publics. In the words of the PRSA, "Public relations helps an organization and its publics adapt mutually to each other." In practice, however, Lee often engaged in one-way propagandizing on behalf of clients despised by the public, including robber baron John D. Rockefeller.

Bernays was the profession's first theorist. A nephew of Sigmund Freud, Bernays drew many of his ideas from Freud's theories about the irrational, unconscious motives that shape human behavior. Bernays saw public relations as an "applied social science" that uses insights from psychology, sociology, and other disciplines to scientifically manage and manipulate the thinking and behavior of an irrational and "herdlike" public. "The conscious and intelligent manipulation of the organized habits and opinions of the masses is an important element in democratic society," he wrote in Propaganda. "Those who manipulate this unseen mechanism of society constitute an invisible government which is the true ruling power of our country."

According to the U.S. Bureau of Labor Statistics, public relations specialists held approximately 122,000 jobs in 1998, while there were approximately 485,000 advertising, marketing, and public relations managers working in all industries. Modern public relations uses a variety of techniques including opinion polling and focus groups to evaluate public opinion, combined with a variety of high-tech techniques for distributing information on behalf of their clients, including satellite feeds, the Internet, broadcast faxes, and database-driven phone banks to recruit supporters for a client's cause.

The skills and techniques used to manage the public have also expanded over the years. According to the PRSA, "Examples of the knowledge that may be required in the professional practice of public relations include communication arts, psychology, social psychology, sociology, political science, economics, and the principles of management and ethics. Technical knowledge and skills are required for opinion research, public issues analysis, media relations, direct mail, institutional advertising, publications, film/video productions, special events, speeches, and presentations."

Although public relations professionals are stereotypically seen as coporate servants, the reality is that almost any organization that has a stake in how it is portrayed in the media employs at least one PR manager. Large enough organizations may even have dedicated communications departments. Government agencies, trade associations, and other nonprofit organizations commonly carry out PR activities.

Public relations should be seen as a management function in any organization. An effective communication, or public relations, plan for an organization is developed to communicate to an audience (whether internal or external publics) in such a way the message coincides with organizational goals and seeks to benefit mutal interests whenever possible.

A number of specialties exist within the field of public relations, including:

— crisis management

— reputation management

— issue management

— investor relations and labor relations

— grassroots PR (sometimes referred to as astroturf PR)

Also, many large agencies separate their work into area-specific "practices," while smaller agencies specialize in only one or a few:

— foodservice PR

— healthcare PR

— technology PR

— public affairs PR

— online PR

There are disciplines with public relations functions that, though closely related to PR, have differing and unique characters and goals.

Marketing and Advertising

While public relations generally tries to influence the

public's perceptions and behavior in a variety of ways and arenas, marketing concentrates on influencing the public to buy goods and services. Advertising is an important tool for marketers, though not the only one. As in other areas of PR, publicity events are also used, and, if used correctly, generate enough "buzz" and free media coverage that would be impossible or impractical to replicate with a traditional advertisement.

Propaganda

Propaganda is certainly an area of public relations, albeit a far less nuanced one. PR most often tries to convince the public of something using a wide array of intellectual and emotional tools, while propaganda usually relies on visceral emotions like love, fear, loyalty, prejudice, and others, to control a population. If the population can be convinced (as is often the case), so much the better for the propagandist, but achieving control is the primary objective of propaganda, with or without the audience's "hearts and minds."

A few influential propaganda pieces include the film "*Triumph des Willens*" ("Triumph of the Will"), made by Nazi-era filmmaker Leni Riefenstahl. It is widely considered the best propaganda film ever made, both for its effect on the German people and for its artistry. Another instrument they used was a fraudulent document entitled "Protocols of the Elders of Zion" that seemingly detailed a Jewish plot to take over the world. The "Protocols" were a major factor in whipping up anti-Semitic fervor in Germany, and had earlier also been very effective in Russia. In the US they had been popularized by Henry Ford in a book that would later be cited by Adolf Hitler.

On the American side of World War II were the Four Freedoms by Norman Rockwell, a series of four paintings that were meant to motivate Americans to fight to preserve four basic freedoms outlined in a speech by President Franklin D. Roosevelt: freedom of speech, freedom of worship, freedom from want, and freedom from fear. The "Why We Fight" films, produced by Frank Capra, were also influential.

Audiences and Stakeholders

The most fundamental rule in public communications is to know who one's audience is, and to tailor every message to appeal to that audience. An "audience" can be a general, nationwide or worldwide audience, but it is more often a segment of a population. Marketers often refer to economy-driven "demographics," such as "white males 18-49," but in public relations an audience is more fluid, being whoever the client wants to reach. In addition to audiences, there are usually stakeholders, literally people who have a "stake" in a given issue. All audiences are stakeholders (or presumptive stakeholders), but not all stakeholders are audiences.

For example, a charity commissions a PR agency to create an advertising campaign to raise money to find a cure for a disease. The charity and the people with the disease are stakeholders, but the audience is anyone who likely to donate money. Sometimes the interests of differing audiences and stakeholders common to a PR effort necessitate the creation of several distinct but still complementary messages. This is not always easy to do, and sometimes—especially in politics —a spokesperson or client says something to one audience that angers another audience or group of stakeholders.

The Press Conference

A press conference consists of someone speaking to the media at a predetermined time and place. Press conferences usually take place in a public or quasi-pubiic place. Press conferences provide an excellent opportunity for speakers to control information and who gets it; depending on the circumstances, speakers may hand-pick the journalists they invite to the conference instead of making themselves available to any journalist who wishes to attend.

It is also assumed that the speaker will answer journalists' questions at a press conference, although they are of course not obligated to. However, someone who holds several press conferences on a topic (especially a scandal) will be asked questions by the press, regardless of whether they indicate they will entertain them, and the more conferences the person holds, the more aggressive the questioning may become. Therefore, it is in a speaker's interest to answer journalists' questions at a press conference to avoid appearing as if they have something to hide.

But questions from reporters—especially hostile reporters —detracts from the control a speaker has over the information they give out. For even more control, but less interactivity, a person may choose to issue a press release. A press release is simply a written statement distributed to the media. It is a fundamental tool of PR work. The typical press release announces that the statement is "FOR IMMEDIATE RELEASE" across the top, and lists the issuing organization's media contacts directly below. The media contacts are the people that the release's issuer wants to make available to the media; for example, a press release about new scientific study will typically list the study's lead scientist as its media contact.

The text of the press release is usually (but not always) written as a news story, with an eye-catching headline and an article written in standard journalistic inverted pyramid style. This style is effective for reaching harried, and often skeptical journalists who rarely read entire releases. It also makes it easy for journalists to lift entire passages from a release and insert them into their own article. While this practice is frowned upon in newsrooms, journalism is a deadline-driven industry, and it is not uncommon for reporters to occasionally copy or modify a line or two from a press release. PR practitioners, on the other hand, design releases to encourage as much "lifting" as possible, so in essence, the less professional a journalist is, the more successful the release is judged to be.

Press releases are usually sent via a Newswire service (such as PR Newswire) to media outlets. PRESS RELEASES ARE an ideal way for organizations to control the information they give to the media. Very often the information in a press release finds its way verbatim, or minimally altered, to print and broadcast reports. If a media outlet reports that "John Doe said in a statement today that...", the "statement" was almost always a press release.

However, because press releases reflect their issuer's preferred interpretation or packaging of a story, journalists are often skeptical of their contents. Of course, the level of skepticism, if any, depends on what the story is and who's telling it. Newsrooms receive so many press releases that, unless it is a story that the media are already paying attention to, a press release alone isn't always enough to catch a journalist's attention.

"The Circuit"

The "circuit" generally refers to the "talk show circuit." A PR spokesperson (or his/her client) "does the circuit" by being interviewed on television and radio talk shows with audiences that the client wishes to reach.

The Rolodex'

After a PR practitioner has been working in the field for a while, he or she accumulates a list of contacts in the media and elsewhere in the public affairs sphere. This "Rolodex" becomes a prized asset, and job announcements sometimes even ask for candidates with an existing Rolodex, especially those in the media relations area of PR.

Political campaigns are peak times for defining one's opponents, though the process occurs continually. In the most recent U.S. presidential campaign, George W. Bush defined John Kerry as a "flip-flopper," among other characterizations. In 1996, President Bill Clinton seized upon opponent Bob Dole's promise to take America back to a simpler time, promising in contrast to "build a bridge to the 21st century." This painted Dole as a person who was somehow opposed to progress.

But organizations and other groups of people can be defined just as easily as candidates. In the debate over abortion, pro-abortion rights groups defined their opponents by defining themselves instead: "pro-choice." Anti-abortion rights groups responded in kind, branding themselves "pro-life." Extrapolating their respective rhetorics, pro-choice groups refer to their opponents as "anti-choice," and pro-life groups refer to their opponents as "pro-abortion."

More recently, opponents of same-sex marriage in the U.S. have declared that their opponents are not the gay couples suing for the right to marry in various state courts, but rather the judges who rule in their favor. They are now called "activist judges," implying that they impose their personal beliefs instead of objectively interpreting the law. This sidesteps the thorny issue of making millions of gay people an "enemy," and instead focuses attention on the much smaller judiciary, who all Americans can ostensibly agree should be prevented from being "activists" on the bench.

Managing Language

If a politician or organization can use an apt phrase in relation to an issue, such as in interviews or news releases, the news media will often repeat it verbatim, thus furthering the message. "New Deal" became a description of President Franklin D. Roosevelt's anti-Depression economic plans, and "states' rights/state sovereignty" became near-code words for anti-civil rights legislation. Recent examples come almost solely from Republican politicians: "death tax" for estate tax, "racial preferences" for affirmative action, "faith-based" instead of religious, and several others.

A famous saying goes "Any publicity is good publicity," and celebrities tend to be fans of this dictum. If a celebrity says or does something embarrassing, he or she will often turn it into a strength and make it part of his or her "image." Of course, this tactic is used just as much with favorable situations as much as with unfavorable ones.

A current example involves the entertainer Jessica Simpson, who gained nationwide prominence when she wondered aloud on a reality show if "Chicken of the Sea"-brand tuna fish was actually chicken or tuna, garnering her a reputation for being slow-witted. But by the summer of 2004, she was being paid to endorse a brand of breath mints called "Liquid Ice." In the product's television commercial, Simpson replicates her earlier confusion by debating whether the mint is really liquid or ice. So although she was previously ridiculed, she (and her advisors) turned her nationwide embarrassment into a lucrative endorsement deal.

Ethical and Social Issues

Many of the techniques used by PR firms are drawn from the institutions and practices of democracy itself. Persuasion, advocacy, and education are instruments through which individuals and organizations are entitled to express themselves in a free society, and many public relations practitioners are engaged in practices that are widely considered as beneficial, such as publicizing scientific research, promoting charities, raising awareness of public health concerns and other issues in civil society.

However, a number of strong criticisms of public relations have been made over the years. One of the most controversial practices in public relations is the use of front groups—organizations that purport to serve a public cause while actually serving the interests of a client whose sponsorship may be obscured or concealed. The creation of front groups is an example of what PR practitioners sometimes term the third party technique—the art of "putting your words in someone else's mouth." PR Watch, a nonprofit organization that monitors deceptive PR activities, has published numerous examples of this technique in practice.

Current issues in ethical and social arenas have been brought to the attention of people from all stratas of the population when it was determined that more than one journalist with a platform had received money from a Public Relations firm for espousing a certain point of view.

Publicity

Publicity is one of the variables that comprise the promotional mix. The other components of promotions are advertising, sales promotion, and personal selling. Promotion is one of the variables that comprise the marketing mix. The other three are product management, pricing, and distribution. Publicity is closely related to public relations. Whereas public relations is the management of all communications between the firm and the general public, publicity is the management of product or brand related communications between the firm and the general public. It is primarily an informative activity (as opposed to a persuasive one), but its ultimate goal is to promote the companies products, services, or brands. A publicity plan is a planned program aimed at obtaining favorable press coverage for a companies products.

The most basic tool of the publicist is the press release, but other techniques include telephone press conferences, in-studio media tours, multi-component video news releases (VNR's), newswire stories, and internet releases. For these releases to be used by the media, they must be of interest to the public (or at least to the market segment that the media outlet is targeted to). The releases are often customized to match the media vehicle that they are being sent to. Getting noticed by the press is all about saying the right thing at the right time. A publicist is continuously asking what about you or your company will pique the reader's curiosity and make a good story?

An example is if three people die of water poisoning, an alert publicist would release stories about the technology embodied in a water purification product. But the publicist cannot wait around for the news to present opportunities. They must also try to create their own news. Examples of this include:

— Contests

— Walkathons

— Art exhibitions

— Event sponsorship

— Arrange a speech or talk

— Make an analysis or prediction

— Conduct a poll or survey

— Issue a report

— Take a stand on a controversial subject

— Arrange for a testimonial

— Announce an appointment

— Celebrate an anniversary

— Invent then present an award

— Stage a debate

— Organize a tour of your business or projects

— Issue a commendation

13

Two-Step Flow of Communication Theory

Man has forever fought against the forces of entropy, working very diligently at creating order and meaning, dissecting and perusing until order is achieved. For civilization this has been important. It has lent the world many fascinating theories about our surroundings and the effect human beings can have. As order driven beings, we seek to stretch and apply knowledge gained in all aspects of life to situations and experiences very different from the origin of the knowledge. It is through the stretching and manipulating of old thought that new insights are made, and new psychological mountains are tackled. It is through this stretching and manipulating of one socio-political based theory that the field of Advertising has defined some of its capabilities and constraints in the area of mass communication. This theory involves the two-step flow of communication.

As with most theories now applied to Advertising, the Two-step flow of communication was first identified in a field somewhat removed from communications-sociology. In 1948, Paul Lazarsfeld, Bernard Berelson, and Hazel Gaudet published The People's Choice, a paper analyzing the votersi decision-making processes during a 1940 presidential election campaign. The study revealed evidence suggesting that the flow of mass communication is less direct than previously supposed. Although the ability of mass media to reach a large audience, and in this case persuade individuals in one direction or another, had been a topic of much research since the 1920's, it was not until the People's Choice was published that society really began to understand the dynamics of the media-audience relationship. The study suggested that communication from the mass media first reaches "opinion leaders" who filter the information they gather to their associates, with whom they are influential. Previous theories assumed that media directly reached the target of the information. For the theorists, the opinion leader theory proved an interesting discovery considering the relationship between media and its target was not the focus of the research, but instead a small aspect of the study.

Lazarsfeld et al suggested that "ideas often flow from radio and print to the opinion leaders and from them to the less active sections of the population." People tend to be much more affected in their decision making process by face to face encounters with influential peers than by the mass media. As Weiss described in his 1969 chapter on functional theory, "*Media content can be a determining influence*.... What is rejected is any conception that construes media experiences as alone sufficient for a wide variety of effects." The other piece i00000n the communication process is the opinion leader with which the media information is discussed.

A study by Robert Merton revealed that opinion leadership is not a general characteristic of a person, but rather limited to specific issues. Individuals who act as opinion leaders on one issue, may not be considered influentials in regard to other issues (Merton, 1949). A later study directed by Lazarsfeld and Katz further investigated the characteristics of opinion leaders. This study confirmed the earlier assertions that personal influence seems more important in decision making than media. Again, influential individuals seem constrained in their opinion leading to particular topics, non-overlapping among the individuals. The opinion leaders seem evenly distributed among the social, economical, and educational levels within their community, but very similar in these areas to those with whom they had influence.

Katz and Lazarsfeld did not identify any particular traits amongst opinion leaders that stand out. The traits that characterize each of the opinion leaders in their niche did have things in common, though. For one thing, the opinion leaders were identified as having the strongest interest in their particular niche. They hold positions within their community affording them special competence in their particular niches. They are generally gregarious, sociable individuals. Finally, they had/have contact with relevant information supplied from outside their immediate circle. Interestingly enough, Katz and Lazarsfeld observed that the opinion leaders receive a disproportionate amount of their external information from media appropriate to their niche.

Critical Approach

Although the theory of indirect flow of information from media to the target was quickly adopted, the original study performed by Lazarsfeld, Berelson, and Gaudet was not. It had a few faults. The panel method by which they attempted to better understand the influences reaching a voter was unfaulted. It very effectively allowed the researchers to notice changes in a voter's feelings almost immediately. The resulting unit of change was an objective measurement that could easily be recorded and compared. The faults lie in the manner with which the researchers addressed the flow of influences.

Since the research was not designed to specifically test the flow of influence, the experiment was decidedly lacking in explanations. The first problem concerning the findings of the study were that the data had to be collected in a random sample, but subjects in a random sample can only speak for themselves. For these reasons, each person could only say whether or not they considered his/herself an advice giver.

Lazarsfeld and his associates in the 1940 election study were unable to determine the specific flow of influence. They determined there were a number of opinion leaders spread throughout the socio-economic groups; however, these leaders were not directly linked to particular groups within the socio-economic levels. Even within studies specifically designed to determine who opinion leaders are and how they are different from the average populace, there have been problems born from experimental design. "The criticisms of the concept of opinion leaders has focused mainly on its methodological deficiencies."

Supportive Approach

Although the empirical methods behind the two-step flow of communication were not perfect, the theory did provide a very believable explanation for information flow. The opinion leaders do not replace media, but rather guide discussions of media. Brosius explains the benefits of the opinion leader theory well in his 1996 study of agenda setting, "The opinion leaders should not be regarded as replacing the role of interpersonal networks but, in fact, as reemphasizing the role of the group and interpersonal contacts."

Lazarsfeld and his associates detailed five characteristics of personal contact that give their theory more validity:

- Non-purposiveness/casualness One must have a reason for tuning into a political speech on television, but political conversations can just "pop-up". In this situation, the people are less likely to have their defenses up in preparation, they are more likely open to the conversation.
- Flexibility to counter resistance In a conversation, there is always opportunity to counter any resistance. This is not so in media, a one sided form of communication.
- Trust Personal contact carries more trust than media. As people interact, they are better able through observation of body language and vocal cues to judge the honesty of the person in the discussion. Newspaper and radio do not offer these cues.
- Persuasion without conviction The formal media is forced to persuade or change opinions. In personal communication, sometimes friendly insistence can cause action without affecting any comprehension of the issues.

Menzel introduced another strong point in favor of the two-step flow of information theory. First, there are an abundance of information channels "choked" with all types of journals, conferences, and commercial messages. These are distracting and confusing to their target. With the barrage of information humans are flooded with daily, it is not hard to understand why someone might turn to a peer for help evaluating all of it.

The true test of a theory lies in its timelessness, its ability to spark interest and provoke thought years after its introduction. The two step flow of communication theory has been able to remain relevant throughout the years. This should not be difficult to believe considering it has fueled at least the past few pages this year, forty years after its debut. There have been several recent studies that have addressed issues arising from Lazarsfeld's, Katz's, and Merton's studies from the 1940s. In two such studies Gabriel Weimann and Hans-Bernd Brosius addressed the setting of agendas as a two step flow of communication.

In Weimann's paper addressing the re-emergence of the opinion leader theory into modern day, he addresses several problems that have been overcome sparking the new interest in the old theory. Many researchers have attempted to design credible models for testing the theory, but with only minor success. Brosius and Weimann set out to explain agenda setting using the basis of the two-step flow of communication theory determined by Lazarsfeld, Katz, and the many other researchers. To avoid the difficulties in studying the actual flow of communication, Weimann and Brosius separated the opinion leaders from their two-step flow of communication theory. Participants were studied against a scale to determine the "Strength of Personality".

The Brosius-Weimann study attempts to describe the individuals whose personal communication has impact on agenda setting. These individuals are the archetypal opinion leaders, who still control the flow of information. Weimann and Brosius define agenda setting as a two-step flow, wherein certain individuals (influentials) "collect, diffuse, filter, and promote the flow of information" from media to the community. The difference between these influentials and the opinion leaders, as Weimann stresses, is that these influentials are usually elitists, not spread throughout the community as the old theory suggested. Weimann and Brosius suggest the influentials are a subsection of the opinion leaders.

Applications of the Theory

To those who claim that there are no applications of a

socio-political theory in advertising, exhibit A is the barrage of articles written daily on the very subject. No longer does the advertising industry doubt the existence or qualities of influentials, as they are most commonly referred to today. Instead, the discussion revolves around effectively targeting messages to reach these influentials. For fifty years, the research organization Roper has considered the group of "influentials" important enough to track.

The influentials today seem to be isolated in the upper class. They are the trend-setters. It is this group that is first to adopt new technology, and remains on the leading edge of trends. This is the group that advertising attempts to reach. Daily articles are published on maximizing the market by reaching these influentials. The idea remains that the most efficient media is word-of-mouth, and it is by reaching the influentials with other forms of media that this word-of-mouth is generated. It seems the opinion leaders of yesterday have been overlooked for the smaller subset of influentials.

14

Conversational Technologies

Conversations are an important part of our daily lives. For most people, in fact, they are the most important way to acquire and spread knowledge during a normal working day. Conversations provide a comfortable medium in which knowledge flows in both directions, and where contributors share an inherent context through their subjects and relationships. In addition to old forms of conversations—direct interaction and communication over the phone and in person—conversations are becoming an increasingly important part of the networked world. Witness the popularity of email, chat, and instant messaging, which enable users to increase the range and scope of their conversations to reach those that they may not have before.

Still, little attention has been paid in recent years to the popular Internet channels that most naturally support conversations. Instead, most people see the Web as the driving force, and they view it as a content delivery platform rather than as a place for exchanges among equals. The dominance of the Web has come about because it has succeeded in becoming a fundamentally unifying technology that provides access to content in all forms and formats. However, it tends toward being a traditional one-way broadcast medium, with the largest base of users being passive recipients of content. Conversations have a stubborn way of reemerging in any human activity, however. Recently, much of the excitement and buzz around the Web have centered on sites that use it as a conversational medium. These conversations take place within a particular web site (Slashdot, eBay, Amazon.com) or an application (Napster, AIM/ICQ, Netshow).

And repeating the history of the pre-Web Internet, the new conversations sprout up in a disjointed, chaotic variety where the left hand doesn't know what the right hand is doing. The Web was a godsend for lowering the barrier to access information; it increased the value of all content by unifying the technologies that described and delivered that content. In the same way, Internet conversations stand to benefit significantly by the introduction of a common platform designed to support the rich dynamic and flexible nature of a conversation. Jabber could well become this platform. It's not a single application (although Jabber clients can be downloaded and used right now) nor even a protocol. Instead, using XML, Jabber serves as a glue that can tie together an unlimited range of applications that tie together people and services. Thus, it will support and encourage the growth of diverse conversational systems—and this moment in Internet history is a ripe one for such innovations.

Conversations and Peers

What conversation is? A quick search using Dictionary.com reveals the following:

> con·ver·sa·tion (kän-v r-'sá-sh n) n. 1. A spoken exchange of thoughts, opinions, and feelings; a talk. 2. An informal discussion of a matter by representatives of governments, institutions, or organizations. 3. Computer Science. A real-time interaction with a computer.

Essentially, a conversation is the rapid transfer of information between two or more parties. A conversation is usually characterized by three simple traits: it happens spontaneously, it is transient (lasting a short time), and it occurs among peers—that is, all sides are equal contributors.

Let's turn then to the last trait. The term "peer" is defined by Dictionary.com:

> peer (pîr) n. 1. A person who has equal standing with another or others, as in rank, class, or age; children who are easily influenced by their peers.

The Internet expands this definition to include both people (P) and applications (A). Inherently, when peers exchange information, it is a conversation, since both sides are equal and are transiently exchanging information with each other. Person-to-person conversations (P-P) include email, chat, and message boards. But crucial conversations also include application-to-application (A-A) ones such as web services, IP routing, and UUCP. Least common, but most intriguing for future possibilities, are person-to-application (P-A) conversations such as smart agents and bots. It's interesting to take a step back and look at the existing conversations happening on the Internet today. How well does each technology map to the kind of natural conversational style we know from real life? Let's identify a few important metrics to help evaluate these traditional forms of Internet communication as conversational channels:

— *Time* : The more rapidly messages can be created and delivered, and the more rapidly the recipient can respond, the more productive the conversation is for both participants.

— *P-A* : A technology provides greater potential for future innovation if it inherently supports applications as well as people.

— *Peers* : Participants in a conversation should be equal and the conversation bidirectional.

— *Distributed* : Conversations may be constrained if there is a central form of control or authority.

We can now evaluate a few technologies along some of the metrics just defined.

Email comes to mind first as the most popular form of conversation now happening on the Internet. It is relatively fast, each message taking typically between 30 seconds and a few days to deliver, but certainly not real-time. It is predominantly P-P, with some P-A applications, but it is not a very natural use for A-A, because it provides no structure for content. Usenet is similar to email but is focused on group discussions. Both are innately distributed, and participants are peers. Internet Relay Chat (IRC) is a very popular conversational medium, primarily supporting real-time group discussions. As with email, it's primarily P-P with some P-A and very little A-A. Participants are peers. IRC is a distributed application within a network of groups, but it is restricted to that particular network—it does not extend beyond a single collection of groups.

The traditional Web is real-time, but in a strict sense it does not support conversations, because the participants are not peers. The content may be produced by a person, but it has a natural flow in only one direction. Applications that support conversations can be built and made available on the Web, but they are pretty rigid—each conversation is specific and centralized to that application. The next-generation Web—also called the Two-Way Web by visionary developer Dave Winer—is represented by Microsoft's .NET; and it tries to solve the shortcomings in the evolution of the Web. It involves personal/fractional-horsepower (specialized) HTTP and DAV servers. These systems more naturally support peers and conversations than the traditional Web, but the conversations between these peers are still predominantly one-way (consumer or producer) and are often centralized based on the application or content.

Traditional instant messaging services, such as AOL Instant Messenger, ICQ, Yahoo! Messenger, and MSN Messenger, come the closest to a real-world conversation yet, and that is the reason for their soaring popularity. They unfortunately focus primarily on P-P. The most significant drawback is that they are commercial and completely centralized around a single closed service. You must be part of the service to communicate with others on it.

None of these existing technologies provides a common platform for Internet conversations as the Web does for content. Each is either limited in some important dimension or is specific to one application. A look back at a bit of the World Wide Web's brief history proves quite interesting and enlightening. Back in its pioneering days, the Web was idealized as a revolutionary peer platform that would enable anyone on the Internet to become a publisher and editor. It empowered individuals to publish their unique collections of knowledge so that they were accessible by anyone. The vision was of a worldwide conversation where everyone could be both a voice and a resource.

Although the Web fulfills this vision for many people, it has quickly evolved into a traditional consumer/ producer relationship. If it had instead evolved as intended, we might be in a different world today. Instead of passively receiving content, we might be empowered individuals collectively producing content, publishing parts of ourselves online to our family and friends, and collectively editing the shared knowledge within our communities. So where did it go wrong in this respect? It could be argued that the problem was technological, in that the available tools were browsing-centric, and it wasn't easy to become an editor or publisher.

A more thought-provoking answer might be that the problem was social, in that there was little demand for those empowering tools. Perhaps only a few people were ready to become individual publishers, and the rest of society wasn't ready to take that step. The Web did not stagnate, however. It continued to evolve from a content distribution medium to an application distribution medium. Few users are publishing content, but a huge number of companies, groups, and talented individuals are building dynamic applications with new characteristics that reach beyond the original design of the Web. The most exciting of these exhibit characteristics of a peer medium and empower individuals to become producers as well as consumers. Examples include eBay, Slashdot, IMDB, and MP3.com.

Although the applications provide a new medium for conversations between P-P peers, the mechanisms for doing so are application-specific. These new web-driven peer applications also have the drawbacks of being centralized, of not being real-time in the sense of a conversation, and of requiring their own form of internal addressing. So instead of the Web being used primarily as a peer publishing medium, it has become a client/server application medium upon which a breed of peer applications are being built. Elsewhere in the computer field we can find still other examples of systems that are incorporating greater interactivity. Existing desktop applications are evolving in that direction. They are becoming Internet-aware as they face competition from web sites, so that they can take advantage of the Internet in order to remain competitive and provide utility to the user. Thus, they are evolving from static, standalone, self-contained applications into dynamic, networked, componentized services.

Microsoft, recognizing the importance of staying competitive with online services, is pushing the evolution of desktop applications with their .NET endeavor. By turning applications into networked services, .NET blurs the lines even further between the desktop and the Internet. The evolution of the Web and the desktop shows a definite trend towards applications becoming peers and having conversations with other applications, services, and people. The common language of conversations in both mediums is XML. As a way of providing a hierarchical structure and a meaningful context for data, XML is being adopted worldwide as the de facto language for moving this data between disparate applications.

JABBER

To fully realize the potential for unifying the conversations ranging throughout the Internet today, and enabling applications and services to run on top of a common platform, a community of developers worldwide has developed a set of technologies collectively known as Jabber. Jabber was designed from the get-go for peer conversations, both P-P and particularly A-A, and for real-time as well as asynchronous/offline conversations. Jabber is fully distributed, while allowing a corporation or service to manage its own namespace. Its design is a response to the popularity of the closed IM services.

Jabber began in early 1998 out of a desire to create a truly open, distributed platform for instant messaging and to break free from the centralized, commercial IM services. The design began with XML, which we exploited for its extensibility and for its ability to encapsulate data, which lowers the barrier to accessing it. The use of XML is pervasive across Jabber, allowing new protocols to be transparently implemented on top of a deployed network of servers and applications. XML is used for the native protocol, translated to other formats as necessary in order to communicate between Jabber applications and other messaging protocols.

The Jabber project emerged from that early open collaboration of numerous individuals and companies worldwide. The name Jabber symbolizes its existence as numerous independent projects sharing common goals, each building a part of the overall architecture. These projects include:

— A modular open source server written in C

— Numerous open source and commercial clients for nearly every platform

— Gateways to most existing IM services and Internet messaging protocols

— Libraries for nearly every programming language

— Specialized agents and services such as RSS and language translations

Jabber is simply a set of common technologies that all of these projects agree on collaboratively when building tools for peer-to-peer systems. One important focus of Jabber is to empower conversations between both people and applications.

The Jabber team hopes to create an open medium in which the user has choice and flexibility in the software used to manage conversations, instead of being hindered by the features provided by a closed, commercial service. We hope to accelerate the development of peer applications built on an open foundation, by enabling them to have intelligent conversations with other people and applications, and by providing a common underlying foundation that facilitates conversations and the accessibility of dynamic data from different services.

Centrality of XML

Fundamentally, Jabber enables software to have conversations in XML. When people use Jabber-based software as a messaging platform to have conversations with other people, data exchanges use XML under the surface. Applications use Jabber as an XML storage and exchange service on behalf of their users. XML is not only the core format for encoding data in Jabber; it is also the protocol, the transport layer between peers, the storage format, and the internal data model within most applications. XML permeates every conversation.

The Jabber architecture is also aware of XML namespaces, which permit different groups of people to define different sets of XML tags to represent data. Thus, using a namespace, one group (Dublin Core) has developed a set of tags for talking about the titles, authors, and other elements of a document. Another group might define a namespace for describing music. An instant messaging community using Jabber could combine the two namespaces to exchange information on books about music.

Here is a simple message using Jabber's XML format:

```
<message to="hamlet@denmark" from="horatio@denmark"
type="chat">
 <body>Here, sweet lord, at your service.</body>
</message>
```

And here's a hypothetical message with additional data in a namespace included:

```
<message to="horatio@denmark" from="hamlet@denmark">
<body>Angels and Ministers of Grace, defend us!</body>
<prayer xmlns="http://www.grace.org">
<verse>...</verse>
```

```
</prayer>
</message>
```

By supporting namespaces, Jabber enables the inclusion of any XML data in any namespace anywhere within the conversation. This allows applications and services to include, intercept, and modify their own XML data at any point. Jabber is thus reduced to serving as a conduit between peers. Ironically, this lowly status provides the power that Jabber offers to Internet conversations.

Pieces of the infrastructure

While the goal of Jabber is to support other naming conventions and protocols, rather than to create brand-new ones, it depends on certain new concepts that require new types of syntax and binding technologies. These help create a common architecture.

Identity

Naming is at the heart of any system--each resource must have a unique identity. In Jabber, each resource is identified by a three-part name consisting of a user, a server, and a resource. The user is often an individual, and the server is a system that runs a Jabber-based application. In a name, the user and server are formatted just like email, user@server. This provides a general way to pass identification between people that is already well understood and socially accepted. Since the server resolves the username, the format also allows a user's identity to be managed by a service or corporation the way America Online and Napster manage their usernames. This is an important point for Internet services that are providing a public utility to consumers or companies, and especially for corporations that want to or are required to manage their identities very carefully. This also allows any user to use a third party, such as Dynamic DNS Network Services, for transient access to a permanent hostname so as not to be forced to rely on someone else's identity.

The server component of the identity could also provide a community aspect to naming, as it may be shared between a small group of friends, a family, or a special interest group. The name then stands out and identifies the user's relationship as part of that community. The third part of the identity is the resource. As in a Unix filename or URL, the resource follows the server and is delimited by a slash, as in user@server/resource. Outside Jabber, the name is formatted like a combination of an email address and a web URL: jabber://user@server/resource/data.

This third aspect of the identity, the resource, allows any Jabber application to provide public access to any data within itself, analogous to a web server providing access to any file it can serve. It also serves to identify different applications that might be operating for a single user. For example, my Jabber ID is jer@jabber.org, and when I'm online at home my client application might be identified as jer@jabber.org/desktop.

Presence

Presence is a concept fundamental to conversations, because it supports the arbitrary coming and going of participants. Technically, presence is simply a state that a user or application is in. Traditional states in instant messaging include online, offline, and somewhere in between (away, do not disturb, sleeping, etc.). The Jabber architecture automatically manages presence information for users and applications, distributing the information as needed while strictly protecting privacy. It is often this single characteristic that adds the most value to the peers in a conversation: just knowing that the other peer is available to have a conversation.

Presence can go beyond simple online/offline state information. XML could be used to convey location, activity, and contextual (work/project) or application-specific data. Presence information itself provides an inherent context for P-P conversations, as well as status and location context for A-A conversations. Here is a simple presence example in XML:

```
<presence from="hamlet@denmark">
 <show>away</show>
 <status>Gone to England</status>
</presence>
```

Roster

Another powerful feature of a traditional instant messaging service is the buddy list or roster. The importance of this list is often underestimated. It is a valuable part of the user's reality that they've stored and made available to their applications. In social terms, each user's roster is his or her community. It defines the participants in this community or relationships to larger communities. A roster is an actualization of personal trust and relationships with peers. Applications should use this list intelligently to share their functionality and filter conversations. The circle of trust in which a user has chosen to include his or her computer is a starting point for applications to locate other devices the user utilizes. It should also be used for choosing to collaborate with the resources available from trusted peers.

Architecture

The Jabber architecture closely resembles email. Peers are

connected and route data in a chain until it reaches the desired recipient. A client is connected to its server only, and its server is responsible for negotiating the delivery and receipt of that client's data with other servers or networks using whatever protocol is available. All data within the architecture is processed immediately and passed on to the next peer, or stored offline for immediate delivery once that peer is available again. Peers can play traditional client and server roles within the Jabber architecture. Every server acts as a peer with respect to another server, using SRV DNS records to locate the actual server.

Servers also use hostname dialback, independently contacting the sending server to validate incoming data. This prevents spoofing and helps ensure an overall more reliable and secure trust system. All clients are peers with respect to other clients, and, after establishing a conversation with their servers, are able to establish real-time conversations in XML with any other client. Clients can also include or embed a server internally so that they can operate in any role and provide additional flexibility and security.

Protocols

Along with support for all major instant messaging services (AIM, ICQ, MSN, Yahoo!), Jabber is also protocol agnostic. It uses a variety of applications between the endpoints of the conversations to transparently translate the XML data to and from another protocol. In its immediate applications, Jabber's translation capabilities let it support P-P relationships across traditional instant messaging services, IRC, and email. But the same flexibility also allows the construction of A-A bridges, such as transparent access to SIP, IMXP, and PAM applications, as well as access to Jabber's native presence and messaging functionality from those protocols.

Finally, the protocol-agnostic design of Jabber allows it to participate in the exciting evolution of the Web mentioned earlier in the section "Evolving toward the ideal": An evolution including such technologies as WebDAV, the use of XML over HTTP in the SOAP protocol, the RSS service that broadcasts information about available content, and other web services. We hope to set up revolving door access so that HTTP applications can access native Jabber functionality and so that Jabber applications can transparently access conversations happening over HTTP.

Browsing

A recent addition to Jabber is browsing, which is similar to the feature of the same name in the Network Neighborhood on Microsoft systems. Browsing lets users retrieve lists of peers from other peers and establish relationships between peers. It can be used to see what services might be available from a server, as well as what applications and paths of communication a user has made available to other users and their applications. Peers that a user might make available could include their normal instant messaging client (home, work, laptop, etc.), a pager transport, an offline inbox, a cell phone, a PDA, a TV, a scheduling application, a 3-D game, or a word processor. Additionally, XML information can be made browsable by a user or application, so that a user's vCard (verification information), public key, personal recipes, music list, bookmarks, or other XML information could be read by both people and applications. Browsing also allows people and applications to locate public peers, such as other messaging gateways mentioned earlier, web services, group chats, and agents (searching, translation, fortune, announcements, Eliza).

Conversation Management

By centralizing and coordinating all of your conversations via a central identity, the software managing that identity for you may be empowered to act upon incoming conversations and intelligently filter them. This feature can be used to modify the content of a transmission or, even more often, to make decisions about what to do with a conversation when you're not available (store it offline, copy it to a pager, forward it to another account, etc.). The same feature is also useful to manage the conversations between applications. For instance, if you maintain a personal peer and a work-scheduling peer, conversation management software can redirect incoming conversations to the correct agent based on the relationship to the sender stored in the roster. When you have all of your conversations managed by a common identity, they can be managed directly from one single point, enabling you to have more control over your conversations.

15

Human-computer Interaction

Human-computer interaction (HCI) is the study of interaction between people (users) and computers. It is an interdisciplinary subject, relating computer science with many other fields of study and research. Interaction between users and computers occurs at the user interface (or simply interface), which includes both hardware (i.e. peripherals and other hardware) and software (for example determining which, and how, information is presented to the user on a screen).

Interdisciplinary Aspects

Combined with computer science and information technology are fields including:

— Aesthetics

— Anthropology

— Artificial intelligence

— Cognitive science

— Design

— Ergonomics

— Human factors

— Library and information science

— Psychology

— Social Psychology

— Sociology

Goals fo HCI

A basic goal of HCI is to improve interaction between user and computers, by making computers more user-friendly and easier to use. More broadly, HCI is also concerned with

— methodologies and processes for designing interfaces (i.e., given a task and a class of users, design the best possible interface within given constraints, optimizing for a desired property such as learnability or efficiency of use)

— methods for implementing interfaces (e.g. software toolkits and libraries; efficient algorithms)

— techniques for evaluating and comparing interfaces

— developing new interfaces and interaction techniques

— developing descriptive and predictive models and theories of interaction

A long term goal of HCI is to design computers that can be exploited to their fullest potential as instruments that enhance human creativity, liberate the human mind, and improve communication and cooperation between humans.

Professional practitioners in HCI are usually designers concerned with the practical application of design methodologies to real-world problems. Their work often revolves around designing graphical user interfaces and web interfaces.

Researchers in HCI are interested in developing new design methodologies, experimenting with new hardware devices, prototyping new software systems, exploring new paradigms for interaction, and developing models and theories.

Terminology

HCI vs CHI. The acronym CHI (pronounced kai), for computer-human interaction, has been used to refer to this field, perhaps more frequently in the past than now. However, researchers and practitioners now refer to their field of study as HCI (pronounced as an initialism), which perhaps rose in popularity partly because of the notion that the human, and the human's needs and time, should be considered first, and are more important than the machine's. This notion became increasingly relevant towards the end of the 20th century as computers became increasingly inexpensive (as did CPU time), small, and powerful. Since the turn of the millennium, the field of human-centered computing has emerged as an even more pronounced focus on understanding human beings as actors within socio-technical systems.

Usability vs Usefulness. Design methodologies in HCI aim to create user interfaces that are usable, i.e. that can be operated with ease and efficiently. However, an even more basic requirement is that the user interface be useful, i.e. that it allow the user to complete relevant tasks.

Intuitive and Natural. Software products are often touted by marketeers as being "intuitive" and "natural" to use, often simply because they have a graphical user interface. Many researchers in HCI view such claims as unfounded (e.g. a poorly designed GUI may be very unusable), and some object to the use of the words intuitive and natural as vague and/or misleading. For example, some may argue that input through handwriting is natural, while others counter that handwriting is a skill requiring years of training for children to acquire, and thus is very unnatural. Intuitiveness is probably best thought of as a relative notion, rather than being intrinsic to a user interface. Intuitiveness depends on the user's familiarity and previous experiences, and is subject to cultural and other biases. For example, an icon that looks like a garbage can (for deleting files) may be very mysterious looking to someone from a culture that doesn't store garbage in cans. Even a computer mouse and drag-and-drop actions are not intuitive to a user who has never seen or used them before.

Data Density and Information Absorbtion. The rapid growth in the density of computer screen real estate has created an opportunity to accelerate "information absorbtion" to much higher levels. Classic "data density" on a computer is 50-100 data points, recent advances in data visualization enable 1000s of data points to be presented in forms which can be rapidly absorbed. Interfaces such as virtual reality will give further growth the potential density of information presented.

Design Methodologies

A number of diverse methodologies outlining techniques for human-computer interaction design have emerged since the rise of the field in the 1980s. Most design methodologies stem from a model for how users, designers, and technical systems interact. Early methodologies, for example, treated users' cognitive processes as predictable and quantifiable and encouraged design practitioners to look to cognitive science results in areas such as memory and attention when designing user interfaces. Modern models tend to focus on a constant feedback and conversation between users, designers, and engineers and push for technical systems to be wrapped around the types of experiences users want to have, rather than wrapping user experience around a completed system.

User-centered design: User-centered design (UCD) is a modern, widely practiced design philosophy rooted in the idea that users must take center-stage in the design of any computer system. Users, designers, and technical practitioners work together to articulate the wants, needs, and limitations of the .user and create a system that addresses these elements. Often, user-centered design projects are informed by ethnographic studies of the environments in which users will be interacting with the system.

One of the top academic conferences for new research in human-computer interaction, especially within computer science, is the annually held ACM's Conference on Human Factors in Computing Systems, usually referred to by its short name CHI (pronounced kai). CHI is organized by ACM SIGCHI Special Interest Group on Computer-Human Interaction. CHI is a large, highly competitive conference, with thousands of attendants, and is quite broad in scope.

Accessibility

Accessibility is a general term used to describe how easy it is for people to get to, use, and understand things. It is not to be confused with usability which is used to describe how easily a thing can be used by any type of user.

Disabilities

Accessibility is most often used to describe facilities or amenities to assist people with disabilities, as in "wheelchair accessible". This can extend to Braille signage, wheelchair ramps, audio signals at pedestrian crossings, walkway contours, website design, and so on. The disability rights movement advocates for more accessibility.

Various countries have legislation requiring accessibility:

— In the UK, the Disability Discrimination Act 1995 has numerous provisions for accessibility

— In the US, under the Americans with Disabilities Act of 1990, new public and private business construction generally must be accessible. Existing private businesses are required to increase the accessibility of their facilities when making any other renovations in proportion to the cost of the other renovations. The U.S. Access Board is "A Federal Agency Committed to Accessible Design for People with Disabilities." Many states in the US have their own disability laws.

Transportation

In transportation, accessibility refers to the ease of reaching destinations. People who are in places that are highly accessible can reach many other activities or destinations quickly, people in inaccessible places can reach many fewer places in the same amount of time. A measure that is often used is to measure accessibility in a traffic analysis zone *i* is:

$$Accessibility_i = \sum_j Opportunities_j \, f(C_{ij})$$

where:

— i = index of origin zones

— j = index of destination zones

— $f(C_{ij})$ = function of generalized travel cost (so that nearer (or less expensive) places are weighted more than farther or more expensive places).

Art and entertainment

Pieces of music, novels, and other works of art are commonly judged on their accessibility, with some feeling that less-accessible works are superior and some considering them inferior. For instance, serial music is often valued by its creators and others for its high concentration of information while being criticized by Fred Lerdahl and others for being literally unintelligible.

Computer Accessibility

In human-computer interaction, computer accessibility refers to the usability of a computer system by people with disabilities. It is largely a software concern. However, when hardware or software is used to customize a computer for a disabled person, that equipment is known as adaptive technology. There are several types of disabilities that impact computer use:

- Cognitive disabilities, such as dyslexia, ADHD or autism.
- Complete or partial blindness, including color blindness.
- Hearing impairment.
- Motor or dexterity disability such as paralysis, cerebral palsy, or carpal tunnel syndrome.
- Impairments due to old age.

Designing with accessibility in mind can often enhance usability for all users and for automated access to the site, such as by search engines. A key to accessibility is to let people access content in their preferred way. This can benefit fully able users as well as those with disabilities: for example, some people may prefer icons and others may prefer text; even fully able people may want to adjust text sizes depending on their viewing circumstances; search engines, like blind people, generally cannot make much use of graphics.

Different sites will require different degrees of concern for accessibility. For example: a site providing information specific to ADHD would have a lot more need to be easily accessible by people with ADHD than would a site about atomic physics; a government site of general interest or a resource directory for people in crisis would need to take into account as many disabilities as possible, whereas a site selling spectacles probably would have no reason to make itself easily accessible to the totally blind.

Many people with visual impairments or dyslexia will want to change the colours of text or the background to make it easier to read. Many people with dyslexia or ADHD will want to stop moving images on the screen whilst they are reading, as they are easily distracted. People with ADHD may also be confused or distracted by link-rich sites: they can have difficulty when presented with so many options.

Accessibility is strongly related to universal design in that it is about making things as accessible as possible to as wide a group of people as possible. However, products marketed as having benefited from a Universal Design process are often actually the same devices customized specifically for use by people with disabilities. It is rare to find a Universally Designed product at the mass-market level that is used mostly by nondisabled people; Oxo Good Grips housewares are continually held up as an example.

Cognitive disabilities and illiteracy

The biggest challenge in computer accessibility is to make resources accessible to people with cognitive disabilities - particularly those with poor communication skills - and those without reading skills. For starters, site designers should ensure that navigation and content is as plain and simple as appropriate is a useful start; long texts should provide summaries. Texts can be supplemented by symbols, illustrations, comics and photographs. Screen readers are of only limited use, due to the differences between spoken and written language and the complexity of text.

Visual disabilities

Another significant challenge in computer accessibility is to make software usable for people with visual impairment since computers are largely visual devices. For people with poor vision, it is helpful to use large fonts, high-contrast icons etc. supplemented with auditory feedback and screen magnifying software. In the case of blindness, text to speech (screen reader) software is essential.

About 8% of people, mostly males, suffer from some form of colorblindness. In a well-designed user interface, color should not be the only way of distinguishing between different pieces of information. However, the only colours that matter are colours that people with a deficiency might confuse, which generally means red and green and blue and green.

Motor disabilities

Some people may not be able to use a conventional input device, such as the mouse or the keyboard. Therefore it is important for software functions to be accessible using both or either device; ideally, software uses a generic API that permits the use even of highly specialized devices unheard of at the time of software development. Keyboard shortcuts and mouse gestures are ways to achieve this. More specialized solutions like on-screen keyboard's and alternate input devices like joysticks and trackballs are also available.The astrophysicist Stephen Hawking is a famous example of a person suffering from motor disability. He uses special software that allows him to control his computer using his remaining small movement ability. His computer also talks for him.

Aural disability

While sound user interfaces have a secondary role in common desktop computing, usually limited to system sounds as feedback, software producers take into account people who can't hear, either for personal disability, noisy environments, silence requirements or lack of sound hardware. The system sounds like beeps can be substituted or supplemented with flashing parts of the screen or text (akin to close captions).

Web and accessiblity

On the World Wide Web, the W3C has produced specific guidelines for accessibility via the Web Accessibility Initiative (WAI).

The Cascading Style Sheets system has been devised with this in mind, since it gives the reader full control over the appearance of the page.

Laws

In the United States, since 1998, under Section 508 (29 U.S.C. ' 794d) (of Rehabilitation Act), (Federal) agencies must give disabled employees and members of the public access to information that is comparable to the access available to others.

Most web browsers have an option to ignore the font size specified in a webpage, so that the user can circumvent a small font forced upon him or her by a webpage author. However, sometimes a webpage author fails to take into account that users may want to apply such an option and designs a webpage such that applying this option gives poor results, such as too small a distance between lines, disabled scrolling even though texts do not fit in assigned spaces, overlapping texts, etc.

Affordance

Affordance is a term used by perceptual psychologists, also used in the fields of cognitive psychology, environmental psychology, industrial design, and human-computer interaction. The term was first introduced by psychologist James J. Gibson in 1966, then explored more fully in "*The Ecological Approach to Visual Perception*". An affordance is a property of an object, or a feature of the immediate environment, that indicates how that object or feature can be interfaced with. The empty space within an open doorway, for instance, affords movement across that threshold. A couch affords the possibility of sitting down on it.

Gibson originally meant affordance to refer to all "action possibilites" latent in the environment, objectively measureable, and independent of the individual's ability to recognize those possibilities. Further, those action possibilities are dependent on the capabilities of the actor. For instance, a set of steps with risers four feet high does not afford the act of climbing, if the actor is a crawling infant. So affordances must to be measured along with the relevant actors.

In 1988, Donald Norman refined the term to refer to perceived affordance, as opposed to objective affordance. This distinction that makes the concept dependent not only on the physical capabilities of the actor, but his experience, his expectations, his level of attention, his perceptual ability, etc. If an actor steps into a room with a recliner (an armchair) and a softball, Gibson's definition of affordance allows that the actor may toss the recliner and sit on the softball, because that's objectively possible.

Norman's definition of affordance captures the likelihood that the actor will sit on the recliner and toss the softball, because characteristics of the recliner and softball self-explain and self-suggest their own uses. Norman's definition makes the concept of affordance unmeasurable, and therefore out of the realm of science, but much more pertinent to practical design problems. If we can understand this language, then industrial designers can make tools that explain their own functions, and even tools that recommend themselves for some uses and discourage other uses.

Human Action Cycle

The human action cycle is a psychological model which describes the steps humans take when they interact with computer systems. The model was proposed by Donald A. Norman, a scholar in the discipline of human-computer interaction. The model can be used to help evaluate the efficiency of a user interface (UI). Understanding the cycle requires an understanding of the user interface design principles of affordance, feedback, visibility and tolerance.

The human action cycle describes how humans may form goals and then develop a series of steps required to achieve that goal, using the computer system. The user then executes the steps, thus the model includes both cognitive activities and physical activities.

User interface

The user interface is the aggregate of means by which people (the users) interact with a particular machine, device, computer program or other complex tool (the system). The user interface provides means of:

— Input, allowing the users to control the system

— Output, allowing the system to inform the users (also referred to as feedback)

To work with a system, the users need to be able to control the system and assess the state of the system. For example, when driving an automobile, the driver uses the steering wheel to control the direction of the vehicle, and the accelerator pedal, brake pedal and gearstick to control the speed of the vehicle. The driver perceives the position of the vehicle by looking through the windscreen and exact speed of the vehicle by reading the speedometer. The user interface of the automobile is the whole composed of the instruments the driver can use to accomplish the tasks of driving and maintaining the automobile.

The term user interface is often used in the context of computer systems and electronic devices. The user interface of a mechanical system, a vehicle or an industrial installation is often referred to as the human-machine interface (HMI). Older, not gender-neutral version of the term is man-machine interface (MMI). The abbreviation MMI is still in use, but is said to refer to mammal-machine interface. In science fiction, HMI or MMI is sometimes used to refer to what is better described as direct neural interface.

The system may expose several user interfaces to serve different kinds of users. For example, a computerized library database might provide two user interfaces, one for library patrons (limited set of functions, optimized for ease of use) and the other for library personnel (wide set of functions, optimized for efficiency).

Usability

The design of a user interface affects the amount of effort the user must expend to provide input for the system and to interpret the output of the system, and how much effort it takes to learn how to do this. Usability is the degree to which the design of a particular user interface takes into account the human psychology and physiology of the users, and makes the process of using the system effective, efficient and satisfying.

Types of User interfaces

In computer science and human-computer interaction, the user interface (of a computer program) refers to the graphical, textual and auditory information the program presents to the user, and the control sequences (such as keystrokes with the computer keyboard, movements of the computer mouse, and selections with the touchscreen) the user employs to control the program.

Currently the following types of user interfaces are the most common:

- Command-line interfaces, where the user provides the input by typing a command string with the computer keyboard and the system provide output by printing text on the computer monitor.
- Graphical user interfaces, which accept input via devices such as computer keyboard and mouse and provide articulated graphical output on the computer monitor.
- Web-based user interfaces, which accept input and provide output by generating web pages which are transported via the Internet and viewed by the user using a web browser program.

Other types of user interfaces:

- Batch interface is a non-interactive user interface, where the user specifies all the details of the batch job in advance to batch processing, and receives the output when all the processing is done. The computer does not prompt for further input after the processing has started.

—Gesture interfaces are user interfaces which accept input in a form of hand gestures, or mouse gestures sketched with a computer mouse or a stylus.

—Reflexive user interfaces where the users control and redefine the entire system via the user interface alone, for instance to change its command verbs. Typically this is only possible with a very rich graphic user interfaces.

—Tactile interfaces supplement or replace other forms of output with haptic feedback methods.

—Tangible User Interface which places a greater emphasis on touch and physical environment or its element

—Text user interfaces are user interfaces which output text, but accept other form of input in addition to or in place of typed command strings.

—Touch interface is a graphical user interface using a touchscreen display as a combined input and output device.

—Archy, a keyboard-driven user interface by Jef Raskin, arguably more efficient than mouse-driven user interfaces for document editing and programming.

Modality

A modality is a path of communication employed by the user interface to carry input and output. Examples of modalities:

—*Input* - computer keyboard allows the user to enter typed text, digitizing tablet allows the user to create free-form drawing

— *Output* - computer monitor allows the system to display text and graphics (vision modality), loudspeaker allows the system to produce sound (auditory modality)

The user interface may employ several redundant input modalities and output modalities, allowing the user to choose which ones to use for interaction. A mode is a distinct method of operation within a computer program, in which the same input can produce different results depending of the state of the computer program. Heavy use of modes often reduces the usability of a user interface, as the user must expend effort to remember current mode states, and switch between mode states as necessary.

Transparency (computing)

In human-computer interaction, computer transparency is an aspect of user friendliness which prevents the user from worrying about technical details (like installation, updating, downloading or device drivers). For instance, a program that automatically detects the monitor resolution is more transparent compared to one that requests the user to enter it manually.

In computing and networking, a software that supports different logical actions through the same user or application interface is transparent. For example, the Network File System allows users to access files stored on a remote machine as if they were stored locally, through the same file/folder hierarchy.

Similarly, some file systems allow transparent compression and decompression of data, enabling users to store more files on a medium without any special knowledge; other file systems encrypt files transparently. In software engineering, it is also considered good practice to develop or use abstraction layers for database access, so that the same application will work with different databases; here, the abstraction layer allows other parts of the program to access the database transparently. In object-oriented programming, transparency is facilitated through the use of interfaces or header files with different implementations.

Transparency means that any form distributed system should hide its distributed nature from its users, appearing and functioning as a normal centralized system. There are many types of transparency:

— *Access transparency* - Regardless of how resource access and representation has to be performed on each individual computing entity, the users of a distributed system should always access resources in a single, uniform way.

— *Location transparency* - Users of a distributed system should not have to be aware of where a resource is physically located.

— *Migration transparency* - Users should not be aware of whether a resource or computing entity possesses the ability to move to a different physical or logical location.

— *Relocation transparency* - Should a resource move while in use, this should not be noticeable to the end user.

— *Replication transparency* - If a resource is replicated among several locations, it should appear to the user as a single resource.

— *Concurrent transparency* - While multiple users may compete for and share a single resource, this should not be apparent to any of them.

— *Failure transparency* - Always try to hide any failure and recovery of computing entities and resources.

— *Persistence transparency* - Whether a resource lies in volatile or permanent memory should make no difference to the user.

The degree to which these properties can or should be achieved may vary widely. Not every system can or should hide everything from its users. For instance, due to the existence of a fixed speed of light there will always be more latency on accessing resources distant from the user. If one expects real-time interaction with the distributed system, this may be very noticeable.

In user interface design, programming language design, and ergonomics, the principle (or rule) of least astonishment (or surprise) states that, when two elements of an interface conflict or are ambiguous, the behaviour should be that which will least surprise the human user or programmer at the time the conflict arises, because the least surprising behavior will usually be the correct one.

For example, a user interface may have the behaviour that pressing Control-Q causes the program to quit. The same user interface may have a facility for recording macros, or sequence of keystrokes to be played back later, intended to be able to control all aspects of the program. The user may want to record a keystroke sequence with Control-Q as part (most likely the last part) of the macro. The principle of least surprise says that pressing Control-Q while recording a macro should not quit the program (which would surprise the user), but rather to record the keystroke.

Usability testing

Usability testing is a means for measuring how well people can use something (such as a web page, a computer interface, a document, or a device) for its intended purpose. If people have difficulty understanding instructions, manipulating parts, or interpreting feedback, then developers should improve the design and test it again. During usability testing, the aim is to observe people using the product in as realistic a situation as possible, to discover errors and areas of improvement. Designers commonly focus excessively on creating designs that look "cool", compromising usability and functionality. This is often caused by pressure from the people in charge, forcing designers to develop systems based on management expectations instead of people's needs. A designers' primary function should be more than appearance, including making things work with people.

Setting up a usability test involves carefully creating a scenario, or realistic situation, wherein the person performs a list of tasks using the product being tested while observers watch and take notes. Several other test instruments such as scripted instructions, paper prototypes, and pre- and post-test questionnaires are also used to gather feedback on the product being tested.

For example, to test the attachment function of an e-mail program, a scenario would describe a situation where a person needs to send an e-mail attachment, and ask him or her to undertake this task. The aim is to observe how people function in a realistic manner, so that developers can see problem areas, and what people like. The technique popularly used to gather data during a usability test is called a think aloud protocol.

Usability testing generally involves measuring how well test subjects respond in four areas: time, accuracy, recall, and emotional response. The results of the first test are the baseline or control measurement; all subsequent tests are compared to the baseline.

— *Time on Task*—How long does it take people to complete basic tasks? (For example, find something to buy, create a new account, and order the item.)

— *Accuracy* —How many mistakes did people make? (And were they fatal or recoverable with the right information?)

— *Recall*—How much does the person remember afterwards?

— *Emotional Response*—How does the person feel about the tasks completed? (Confident? Stressed? Would the user recommend this system to a friend?)

Interaction

Interaction is a kind of action which occurs as two or more objects have an effect upon one another. The idea of a two-way effect is essential in the concept of interaction instead of a one-way causal effect. Combinations of many simple interactions can lead to surprising emergent phenomena. It has different tailored meanings in various sciences.

Examples of interaction include:

— communications of any sort. More specific example would be two or more people talking to each other, or communications among groups, organisations, nations or states: trade, migration, foreign relations, transportation; etc.

— the feedback during operation of a machines such as a computer or a tool; more specific example would be the interaction between a driver and the position of his or her car on the road: by steering the driver influences this position, by looking this information returns to the driver.

Interactive Communication

In communications, interactive communication occurs when sources take turns transmitting messages between one another. This should be distinguished from transactive communication, in which sources transmit messages simultaneously.

Media

In media, interactivity is a feature of the media in question. As a result of digitalization and convergence the consumption of media is becoming more interactive. In media the strive for interaction is also a cultural trend.

Physics

In physics, an interaction specifically refers to the action of one physical object upon another and results in an interaction energy - the physical objects under consideration may range from point particles to quantum fields. For example, the interaction of charged particles takes place through the mediation of electromagnetic fields, whereas beta decay occurs by means of the weak interaction. There are believed to be four fundamental interactions in Nature.

Sociology

In sociology, social interaction is a dynamic, changing sequence of social actions between individuals (or groups) who modify their actions and reactions due to the actions by their interaction partner(s). Social interactions can be differentiated into:

— accidental - not planned and likely not repeated. For example, asking a stranger for directions or shopkeeper for product availabity.

— repeated - not planned, bound to happen from time to time. For example, accidentaly meeting a neigbour from time to time when walking on your street;

— regular - not planned, but very common, likely to raise questions when missed. Meeting a doorman or a security guard every workday in your workplace, dining every day in the same restaurant, etc.

— regulated - planned and regulated by customs or law, will definetly raise questions when missed. Interaction in a workplace (coming to work, staff meetings, etc.), family, etc.

Most researchers today agree that in many applications a sample size quite larger than five is required to detect a satisfying amount of usability problems.

16

Functional Network Communication

Functional communication networks describe the patterns of communication which evolve among individuals or nodes (i.e., who talks with whom). The unit of analysis in communication networks is not the individual, but rather the relationship between or among individuals. The methodological techniques used to study communication networks include traffic monitoring, studies of task requirements, participant-observation of interactions, cross-sectional surveys, small-world procedures (taking one part as representative of the whole), and studies of message diffusion. The uses to be examined by these methods are production (getting the job done), innovation (exploring new options), and maintenance (keeping the system and its components operational). The functional communications networks can help us to understand information flow within a space organization and between the space organization and external systems.

Internal Communication

Information may flow in several directions within an organizational structure. Communication flowing in different directions serves different functions and is likely to encounter different obstacles or barriers.

Formal communication networks- Formal communication networks reflect management-imposed structures which channel interaction up and down the organizational line and, to a lesser extent, laterally among peers. Formal communication networks are highly important to the management function, and managers spend an average of 75% of their time in communication activities. Communication from managers to subordinates typically assumes one of five types:

1) inculcation of organizational or group goals,

2) explanation of organizational policies and procedures,

3) job rationale,

4) job instruction, and

5) feedback.

As Katz and Kahn note, although a manager's task may be simplified by offering subordinates only job instruction and feedback, more general instruction gives workers a framework for coping with nonroutine conditions and promotes identification with organizational goals. Therefore, the first task of a space manager is to identify and impart the goals of the organization or mission.

Once a communication framework has been established, attention can be turned to using that framework to meet organizational needs. Communication up the line helps managers monitor performance and provides information that is useful for making decisions. Communication down the line provides direction, course changes, and feedback. Although downward communication can be direct, as when top management issues an edict to subordinates at all levels, certain conditions serve as barriers to the upward flow of communication:

— First, role expectations cast subordinates as listeners rather than as communicators.

— Second, since managers control their subordinates' fates, subordinates tend to censor communications which might displease the manager or cast aspersions upon their own performance

— Third, upward communication tends to proceed in a step-by-step fashion.

At each step, someone is in a position to act as a gatekeeper. Although this individual may perform the positive function of preventing information overload, he or she may also filter, distort, or block needed information. In a steep, multilevel hierarchy, it is unlikely that messages from the lowest levels will ever reach the top. Space planners and managers must be aware of these barriers and establish mechanisms to smooth the upward flow of important information.

Horizontal or lateral communication involves the exchange of information among workers at the same hierarchical level. As Katz and Kahn note, horizontal communication eases some of the burdens of management because peers can indoctrinate and train one another, and can coordinate activities of groups of workers. Moreover, horizontal communication provides important and necessary socioemotional rewards.

However, peer indoctrination and training can be faulty or even at cross-purposes to management goals. Some organizations adopt heavy- handed managerial techniques in order to discourage horizontal communication flow. However, this form of cure may be worse than the ailment, particularly under conditions of isolation and confinement. In space as elsewhere, the problem is not one of preventing horizontal communication, but of preventing such communication from assuming destructive forms.

Informal communication networks- In addition to the imposed organizational arrangement, group members construct their own communication networks. These informal networks have two basic purposes. The first function of an informal network is to compensate for inadequacies in the formal network by establishing new links to bypass obstacles that emerge in the formal structure. In many groups there is someone who can expedite the matter at hand; frequently, the expeditor is not the person charged with the responsibility. By locating the right person (who may be anyone in the organization), the informal network is used to serve organizational goals.

A second function of an informal communication network is to serve the needs of the individuals involved, whether or not these needs coincide with the goals of the organization. These informal networks link those with similar interests and experiences (Rogers and Kincaid, 1981) and those who simply like each other.

Informal networks serve a valuable organizational function: they protect the individual from becoming isolated from colleagues of his or her profession by stimulating him or her to more creative thinking and by supplying a psychological support group. It is not unusual for an ongoing, informal work relationship to obscure the formal organizational structure until, finally, the formal is forgotten. Within large spacecrews, we can expect that informal networks will [208] arise. In examining the advantages or problems of an organizational unit, informal communication networks must be considered as carefully as formal communication networks.

Group membership- Different organizational subsystems can constitute themselves into cliques or factions which do not communicate effectively with one another. Members of particular groups may have difficulty identifying or appreciating each others' specific perspectives and goals. The attitudes and behaviors of most subgroups or cliques are strongly influenced by one or a few individuals called opinion leaders. It is important to know who is likely to emerge as an opinion leader in space, and how this individual's influence on other clique members can be directed toward positive and productive interactions with other subgroups. Good communication and cordial relations can be promoted among different groups by having selected individuals maintain simultaneous membership in them.

A person serving this "linking pin" function is likely to understand the needs and views of each group and to be able to represent each to the other. From previous confinement activity, we know that participation in two or more subgroups improves intergroup relations. In the Tektite underwater research project, benefits accrued from having engineers and scientist-aquanauts play active roles in each others' fields of expertise. A third role is that of the liaison, where the individual connects two or more cliques within a system without belonging to any. These roles share many of the same requirements. It would be interesting to determine which role accomplishes certain tasks with the greatest effectiveness and with the least burden on the role occupant. It would also be useful to understand more fully the desired characteristics of individuals occupying such roles.

Performance and satisfaction- The structural arrangement of a communication network can influence its effectiveness. Reviews of experimental nets suggest that when the task is simple and requires people in central positions to collect and distribute messages, centralized nets tend to be an effective arrangement; however, when the task is complex and requires people in central positions to perform numerous and varied operations, decentralized nets tend to be more effective. In terms of member satisfaction, decentralized nets have been found to offer participants greater feelings of self-determination and to provide more socioemotional gratification than do centralized nets.

For instance, the experimental nets examined by Shaw consisted of stations staffed by single unsupported individuals. It is not clear that such findings can be extrapolated to other conditions. Centralized nets could be more effective than decentralized nets even when the task is complex if, for example, the centralized station has higher information-processing capability, as through multiple staffing or data-processing support. In addition, "centralized" and "decentralized" nets are two extreme arrangements. It may be that a preferred system would combine characteristics from each.

To date, spacecrews have been sufficiently small that internal networking considerations have been minimal or nonexistent. However, questions of structuring communication linkages can be expected to grow with the crew and to require more careful analysis in terms of both effectiveness and acceptability.

External Communication

A fundamental difference between space and other organizational arrangements is that informal contacts between the space vehicle and the ground will be severely curtailed. This limitation puts a large burden on the formal communication network.

For the crew of a space vehicle, external communication will assume one of two forms. These are

1) primarily task-oriented communication with ground control, and
2) primarily socioemotional communication with family and friends.

Communication with ground control- The most important requirements of a communication system relate to effectiveness and reliability. However, given an adequately operating system, communication-related problems can still plague the mission-ground relationship.

A primary challenge, then, is to devise a communication arrangement which provides ground control with adequate access to the crew, but which does not interfere unduly in the crew's life space. Systems which allow ground control to "tap in" to the crew at will (and particularly systems which tap in unannounced) can be expected to arouse strong negative reactions. First, surveillance itself decreases autonomy and thereby decreases job satisfaction. Second, communication systems which allow unannounced eavesdropping or rude interruptions may be seen as an unwarranted infringement on the privacy of the group. Third, communication systems which are under the control of outsiders may raise conflicts concerning who is "in charge."

There is also the problem of who on the ground should have access to the crew. Usually communication from ground personnel is relayed through a third party. Yet in a simulation of a Spacelab flight, researchers on the ground found that their ability to collaborate with crewmember experimenters was significantly impaired by this two-step process. Alternately, if many individuals were to have access to the communication system, the aggregated messages could become overly burdensome and interfere with effective communication. Thus, a major problem confronting planners and managers is to devise a system that provides both ground control and spacecrews with an optimal degree of accessibility to each other. This requirement includes providing the crew with some opportunity for private, internal communication.

Communication with family and friends- Personal communication that makes it possible to converse with family and friends has the potential of reducing anxiety concerning events at home and of reducing dependency upon fellow crewmembers for the satisfaction of all interpersonal needs. Extended spaceflight is expected to result in an increased desire to communicate with the folks back home. The Russian experiences have demonstrated that as mission length increases, so do the depth and duration of external communications, some researchers argues that space voyagers should be given ample opportunity to communicate with people who are important to them personally, and that a scrambler system or comparable device should be used to ensure privacy. However, the value of ready access to people at home is not accepted by all. Some writers argue that it is to the advantage of an isolated and confined group that it remain out of contact with friends and relatives.

Some of the problems identified above may represent imperfections in the communication systems themselves. For example, the availability of private communication systems may allow for more spirited messages. Or, the failure of a family member or friend to communicate on time may be less worrisome if communication with home is so routine that it no longer is necessary to arrange each transmission well in advance. Post-communication letdown may be minimized if the next opportunity to communicate is in the near rather than in the distant future.

Mediated communication is generally employed in support of work-related tasks. One would not expect such exchanges to influence face-to-face relationships. In space, mediated communication with family and friends is likely to be emotionally charged and could influence the cohesiveness of the spacecrew. Research on how such communication opportunities could influence primary group relations is needed.

The questions surrounding contact with family and friends at home are among the more complicated interpersonal issues that space planners and space travelers must address. Although our emphasis here is on the spacecrew and their mission, whatever compromises are struck must consider the welfare of those at home as well as those in the space vehicle. There are numerous unanswered questions surrounding communication of persons in space. Within the space capsule, the direct verbal communication among crewmembers may be influenced by attenuation related to transmission characteristics of the capsule environment and by high levels of ambient noise.

Conditions of space (particularly weightlessness) can alter nonlinguistic communication cues such as voice tone, facial expression, and distancing. These variations, especially when complicated by the linguistic and cultural differences of multinational crewmembers, could result in miscommunication and interfere with the efficient work operations or social interactions of space travelers. Studies of international crews such as those proposed for exploring the ocean bottom would offer an opportunity to investigate the implications of linguistic diversity in space. In addition, procedures need to be developed to ensure that verbal messages are received and understood. More generally, greater attention needs to be given to understanding which cues survive and which fail the space environment, as well as the kinds of miscommunication that result from altered cues.

Equally demanding questions involve the establishment and maintenance of working and personal relationships with those on Earth or on other spacecraft. Space planners charged with providing for extended spaceflight face special problems in their attempts to implement communication systems in the face of rapid development in the technology. At the operations level, they must determine how such systems can be designed to avoid overload and to select and prioritize important information. At a more general level, they must determine how these systems can serve the information needs as defined by users and the information needs imposed by mission planners. Questions of protocol and of access must also be addressed.

It is predicted that space travelers, like other users of mediated systems, will find the medium better suited to simple rather than complex tasks and to work related rather than social interactions. Unlike other users, space travelers will not have the option of substituting a direct exchange when they find the medium wanting. Space travel reverses the usual pattern of direct interaction with intimates and mediated interaction with secondary or work related contacts. One of the more important questions for extended spaceflight concerns if, and how, a communication system can be used to deal with the kinds of complex and emotional interactions that are usually reserved for face to face communication.

Space managers, like managers everywhere, must deal with problems of keeping needed communication channels open while discouraging those communication activities which tend to inhibit the goals of the organization. Cliques and factions evolve in all large undertakings; however, negative aspects associated with such subgroups could be particularly destructive in the closed environment of space. A possible solution is the involvement of individuals who share memberships in several groups and who can interpret each group to the other. What is not well known is whether the burden placed on these individuals by their intermediating responsibilities is manageable in the space environment.

The effectiveness and efficiency of operations and the satisfaction of participants have been related to the structure of the communication network. We need to determine whether centralized, decentralized, or some combination of these two arrangements are most appropriate to space and how the efficacy of these arrangements might change over very long periods of time.

A phenomenon which has emerged in many confinement experiences is the tendency of separated individuals to direct hostility to outside contacts. In space, this tendency could translate into problems between on board crewmembers and ground control. Several suggestions, including the use of two way video and the training of ground crews in interpersonal relations, have been advanced. The smooth interaction between the crew and the ground is a fundamental issue which needs to be addressed for extended spaceflight. Whatever solution or range of solutions are adopted must take into consideration both the access needs of the ground and the autonomy needs of the crewmembers.

17

Barriers to Communication

Many of the problems that occur in a organization are the direct result of people failing to communicate. Faulty communication causes the most problems. It leads to confusion and can cause a good plan to fail. Communication is the exchange and flow of information and ideas from one person to another. It involves a sender transmitting an idea to a receiver. Effective communication occurs only if the receiver understands the exact information or idea that the sender intended to transmit.

Studying the communication process is important because you coach, coordinate, counsel, evaluate, and supervise through this process. It is the chain of understanding that integrates the members of an organization from top to bottom, bottom to top, and side to side.

Following factors involved in the communication process:

— *Idea* First, information exists in the mind of the sender. This can be a concept, idea, information, or feelings.

— *Encodes* Next, a message is sent to a receiver in words or other symbols.

— *Decoding* The receiver then translates the words or symbols into a concept or information.

During the transmitting of the message, two processes will be received by the receiver. Content and context. Content is the actual words or symbols of the message which is known as language - spoken and written words combined into phrases that make grammatical and semantic sense. We all use and interpret the meanings of words differently, so even simple messages can be misunderstood. And many words have different meanings to confuse the issue even more.

Context is the way the message is delivered and is known as Paralanguage - tone of voice, the look in the sender's eye's, body language, hand gestures, state of emotion (anger, fear, uncertainty, confidence, etc.). Paralanguage causes messages to be misunderstood as we believe what we see more than what we hear; we trust the accuracy of nonverbal behaviors more than verbal behaviors.

Many leaders think they have communicated once they told someone to do something, "I don't know why it did not get done...I told Jim to it." More than likely, Jim misunderstood the message. A message has NOT been communicated unless it is understood by the receiver. How do you know it has been properly received? By two-way communication or feedback. This feedback will tell the sender that the receiver understood the message, its level of importance, and what must be done with it. Communication is an exchange, not just a give, as all parties must participate to complete the information exchange.

Anything that prevents understanding of the message is a barrier to communication. Many physical and psychological barriers exist. Culture, background, and bias - We allow our past experiences to change the meaning of the message. Our culture, background, and bias can be good as they allow us use our past experiences to understand something new, it is when they change the meaning of the message then they interfere with the communication process.

Noise - Equipment or environmental noise impede clear communication. The sender and the receiver must both be able to concentrate on the messages being sent to each other.

Ourselves - Focusing on ourselves, rather than the other person can lead to confusion and conflict. The "Me Generation" is out when it comes to effective communication. Some of the factors that cause this are defensiveness, superiority, and ego.

Perception - If we feel the person is talking too fast, not fluently, does not articulate clearly, etc., we may dismiss the person. Also our preconceived attitudes affect our ability to listen. We listen uncritically to persons of high status and dismiss those of low status.

Message - Distractions happen when we focus on the facts rather than the idea. Our educational institutions reinforce this with tests and questions. Semantic distractions occur when a word is used differently than you prefer. For example, the word chairman instead of chairperson, may cause you to focus on the word and not the message.

Environmental - Bright lights, an attractive person, unusual sights, or any other stimulus provides a potential distraction.

Smothering - We take it for granted that the impulse to send useful information is automatic. Not true! Too often we believe that certain information has no value to others or they are already aware of the facts.

Stress - People do not see things the same way when under stress. What we see and believe at a given moment is influenced by our psychological frames of references - our beliefs, values, knowledge, experiences, and goals.

These barriers can be thought of as filters, that is, the message leaves the sender, goes through the above filters, and is then heard by the receiver. These filters muffle the message. And the way to overcome filters is through active listening and feedback.

Active Listening

Hearing and listening are not the same thing. Hearing is the act of perceiving sound. It is involuntary and simply refers to the reception of aural stimuli. Listening is a selective activity which involves the reception and the interpretation of aural stimuli. It involves decoding the sound into meaning.

Listening is divided into two main categories: passive and active. Passive listening is little more that hearing. It occurs when the receiver or the message has little motivation to listen carefully, such as music, story telling, television, or being polite.

People speak at 100 to 175 words per minute, but they can listen intelligently at 600 to 800 words per minute (WPM). Since only a part of our mind is paying attention, it is easy to go into mind drift - thinking about other things while listening to someone. The cure for this is active listening - which involves listening with a purpose. It may be to gain information, obtain directions, understand others, solve problems, share interest, see how another person feels, show support, etc. It requires that the listener attends to the words and the feelings of the sender for understanding. It takes the same amount or more energy than speaking. It requires the receiver to hear the various messages, understand the meaning, and then verify the meaning by offering feedback. The following are a few traits of active listeners:

— Spends more time listening than talking.

— Does not finish the sentence of others.

— Does not answer questions with questions.

— Are aware of biases. We all have them...we need to control them.

— Never daydreams or become preoccupied with their own thoughts when others talk.

— Lets the other speaker talk. Does not dominate the conversation.

— Plans responses after the other person has finished speaking.

— Provides feedback, but does not interrupt incessantly.

— Analyzes by looking at all the relevant factors and asking open-ended questions. Walks the person through your analysis.

— Keeps the conversation on what the speaker says.

— Takes brief notes. This forces them to concentrate on what is being said.

FEEDBACK

The purpose of feedback is to change and alter messages so the intention of the original communicator is understood by the second communicator. It includes verbal and nonverbal responses to another person's message.

Providing feedback is accomplished by paraphrasing the words of the sender. Restate the sender's feelings or ideas in your own words, rather than repeating their words. Your words should be saying, "This is what I understand your feelings to be, am I correct?" It not only includes verbal responses, but also nonverbal ones. Nodding your head or squeezing their hand to show